AI from Scratch: A Practical Guide to Building Learning AI

Dedication

This book is dedicated to the countless individuals who have contributed to the field of artificial intelligence, from the pioneers who laid the groundwork to the current generation of researchers and developers pushing the boundaries of what's possible. It's a tribute to their tireless efforts, innovative thinking, and unwavering commitment to advancing our understanding of intelligence, both natural and artificial. Specifically, I dedicate this work to the students, both past and present, whose curiosity and passion for learning have continually inspired me. Their questions, insights, and unwavering enthusiasm for tackling complex problems have been instrumental in shaping my own understanding and approach to teaching AI. This book is a testament to their capacity for growth and their potential to contribute meaningfully to the future of this rapidly evolving field. It is also dedicated to those who have supported me on my journey – my family, colleagues, and mentors – whose unwavering belief in my abilities has empowered me to overcome challenges and pursue my passion for knowledge and education. Without their encouragement and support, this book would not have been possible. Finally, a special dedication goes to the open-source community, whose collaborative spirit and invaluable contributions have made learning and developing AI more accessible to everyone, regardless of their background or resources. Your collective efforts are shaping a more inclusive and vibrant future for AI.

Preface

The field of artificial intelligence is rapidly evolving, presenting both incredible opportunities and significant challenges. This book, "AI from Scratch," aims to provide a practical and accessible pathway for individuals of all backgrounds to enter this exciting domain. It's designed as a hands-on journey, guiding readers from fundamental programming concepts in Python to the construction of sophisticated AI systems. The content is carefully structured to build a solid foundation, starting with the essential tools and libraries and progressively introducing more advanced topics. We won't shy away from the complexities of neural networks, reinforcement learning, and natural language processing, but we will approach these topics with a clear, concise, and engaging style, avoiding unnecessary jargon and emphasizing practical application. Throughout the book, you will encounter numerous projects designed to solidify your understanding and build your practical skills. These range from creating a simple image classifier using the MNIST dataset to developing a functional AI assistant integrating various AI components. These projects are carefully selected to provide a balance of challenge and reward, reinforcing the concepts learned and allowing you to actively apply your knowledge. More than just a collection of technical instructions, this book aims to cultivate an appreciation for the ethical considerations inherent in AI development. We will explore topics such as bias, privacy, and responsibility, encouraging readers to build AI systems not only powerful but also responsible and beneficial to society. While this book offers a comprehensive introduction, it's merely the starting point of your AI journey.
I hope it empowers you to further explore this fascinating field, pushing the boundaries of what's possible and

contributing to the ongoing evolution of artificial intelligence. This book is a reflection of my own experiences teaching and researching in AI. It's a culmination of years of learning, teaching, and collaborating with brilliant minds. The approach is deeply pedagogical, striving to create a supportive and engaging learning environment that encourages curiosity, problem-solving, and creative exploration.

Introduction

Artificial intelligence (AI) is no longer a futuristic concept; it's rapidly transforming our world, influencing everything from the way we communicate and work to how we access information and receive healthcare. Understanding AI is no longer a luxury; it's increasingly becoming a necessity for individuals across numerous disciplines. This book, "AI from Scratch," is your comprehensive guide to navigating this exciting and complex field. Whether you are a computer science student, a data analyst seeking to upskill, or simply an enthusiast with a passion for technology, this book provides a structured and accessible path to mastering the fundamentals of AI and machine learning. We will start with the basics, assuming no prior knowledge beyond fundamental programming skills. We'll guide you through setting up your development environment, mastering essential Python libraries such as TensorFlow, PyTorch, NumPy, Pandas, and Matplotlib, and developing a strong understanding of data science techniques crucial for AI model development. From there, we will progressively explore core concepts such as supervised, unsupervised, and reinforcement learning, demystifying key terms and providing clear, concise explanations. You will learn about the architecture of neural networks, understanding how they learn, how they are trained using algorithms like gradient descent, and how to evaluate their performance. Through practical projects, including building image classifiers and a game-playing AI, you will reinforce your learning and gain hands-on experience. We will delve into advanced architectures such as Convolutional Neural Networks (CNNs), Recurrent Neural Networks (RNNs), and Transformers, illustrating their applications in various AI tasks. We'll also explore the fascinating world of Natural

Language Processing (NLP) and guide you through building an AI assistant as a capstone project. Finally, we will address the crucial ethical considerations surrounding AI development, emphasizing responsible AI practices and the importance of mitigating bias and ensuring privacy. This book is not simply about learning the technical details; it's about fostering critical thinking, problem-solving skills, and a deep understanding of the ethical implications of AI. It's designed to empower you to embark on your own AI journey, contributing to this transformative field and shaping its future.

Installing Python and Essential Libraries

Setting up your AI development environment is the crucial first step in your journey into the world of artificial intelligence. This involves selecting and installing the right tools, understanding their functionalities, and ensuring they work seamlessly together. This section focuses on installing Python, a versatile programming language that forms the bedrock of many AI and machine learning projects, alongside several essential libraries that extend Python's capabilities for data manipulation, visualization, and model building. We'll navigate the installation process for both Python itself and popular packages like Anaconda, TensorFlow, PyTorch, NumPy, Pandas, and Matplotlib, providing guidance to overcome potential hurdles and verification methods to ensure successful installation.

Python, with its clean syntax and extensive libraries, has become the preferred language for many AI developers. Its readability and vast community support make it an excellent choice for beginners and experienced programmers alike. While you can directly install Python from the official website, using a distribution like Anaconda significantly simplifies the process by providing a comprehensive environment that bundles Python along with numerous scientific computing packages, avoiding potential dependency conflicts that often plague manual installations. Anaconda's package manager, conda, allows for effortless installation and management of libraries, further streamlining the development workflow.

To install Anaconda, navigate to the Anaconda website (www.anaconda.com) and download the installer appropriate for your operating system (Windows, macOS, or Linux). The installation process is generally straightforward; just follow the on-screen instructions. Once installed, open the Anaconda Navigator, a graphical user interface that provides access to various applications, including Jupyter Notebook, Spyder, and RStudio. Anaconda's strength lies in its ability to manage different Python environments, preventing clashes between project dependencies. This is especially beneficial when working on multiple projects that might require different versions of libraries. You can create a new environment using the command `conda create -n myenv python=3.9` (replace `myenv` with your desired environment name and `3.9` with your preferred Python version). Activating the environment is done through `conda activate myenv` and deactivating it with `conda deactivate`.

After setting up Anaconda, we'll install the essential libraries. NumPy forms the foundation for numerical computation in Python, providing powerful array operations that are crucial for handling large datasets efficiently. Pandas builds upon NumPy, offering data structures like DataFrames that excel at organizing and manipulating tabular data,
commonly found in machine learning tasks. Matplotlib, a comprehensive visualization library, allows you to create various types of plots to understand your data and visualize model performance. TensorFlow and PyTorch are two leading deep learning frameworks. TensorFlow, developed by Google, is known for its production-level capabilities and vast community support. PyTorch, created by Facebook's AI Research lab, emphasizes flexibility and dynamic computation graphs, making it popular for research and development. The choice between TensorFlow and PyTorch often depends on personal preference and project requirements. Both frameworks offer a range of tools for building, training, and deploying deep learning models.

Installing these libraries through conda is simple. Within your activated Anaconda environment, use the command `conda install -c conda-forge <library name>`, replacing `<library name>` with the desired library (e.g., `numpy`, `pandas`, `matplotlib`, `tensorflow`, `pytorch`). The `-c conda-forge` ensures you're installing from a reputable channel known for its well-maintained packages. Alternatively, you can use pip, Python's package installer. The command `pip install <library name>` installs the library from the Python Package Index (PyPI). However, using conda is generally recommended within an Anaconda environment for better dependency management.

Once the installation is complete, it is essential to verify its success. Open a Python interpreter (either through the Anaconda Navigator or by typing `python` in your terminal) and import the libraries. If no errors occur, it indicates a successful installation. For example:

```python
import numpy as np
import pandas as pd
import matplotlib.pyplot as plt
import tensorflow as tf
import torch
```

If any of these lines raise an `ImportError`, it means the corresponding library is not properly installed or is not accessible within the current environment. Check your installation process and environment configuration to resolve this issue. For TensorFlow and PyTorch, additional verification steps might be necessary, depending on the version and specific hardware configuration. TensorFlow often requires CUDA and cuDNN for GPU acceleration, whereas PyTorch needs similar drivers for optimal performance. Refer to the official documentation for detailed guidance on GPU setup and verification.

Troubleshooting Installation Issues:

During installation, you might encounter various issues. Common problems include network connectivity problems, insufficient permissions, conflicts between different library versions, or issues with incompatible hardware drivers (especially when using GPU acceleration).

Network Connectivity: Ensure your internet connection is stable during the installation process. Intermittent connectivity can interrupt the download and installation of packages.

Permissions: Make sure you have the necessary permissions to write to the installation directory. If you are installing in a system-protected directory, you might need administrator privileges.

Dependency Conflicts: Conda generally handles dependency conflicts efficiently. However, you might occasionally encounter issues. In such cases, it's helpful to create a new, clean environment to avoid conflicts with existing installations. Start by creating a new environment and then installing the libraries within that environment.

Hardware Driver Issues (GPU acceleration): Ensure that you have the correct CUDA and cuDNN drivers installed for TensorFlow and PyTorch if you intend to leverage GPU acceleration. Incorrectly configured drivers can lead to installation failures or runtime errors. Check the TensorFlow and PyTorch websites for specific installation instructions based on your GPU model and CUDA version.

If the problem persists after trying basic troubleshooting steps, consult the relevant documentation, search online forums (such as Stack Overflow), or seek help from the community. Provide detailed information about the error message, your operating system, and the steps you have already taken. Providing clear and comprehensive information is critical for efficient problem-solving.

Beyond the basic installation, exploring the capabilities of each library will unlock the true potential of your AI development environment. NumPy's array operations provide the foundation for efficient numerical computation in machine learning. Practice creating arrays, performing matrix manipulations, and using built-in functions for statistical analysis. Pandas allows efficient data manipulation using DataFrames. Practice loading datasets (e.g., CSV files), cleaning data (handling missing values, converting data types), filtering data based on criteria, and performing aggregations. Matplotlib offers a wide range of plotting capabilities. Experiment with different plot types like scatter plots, histograms, bar charts, and line plots to visualize your data and the performance of your AI models. With TensorFlow and PyTorch, you will build and train your neural networks. Start with simple models and progressively work towards more complex architectures as you learn the fundamentals of deep learning. Remember that consistent practice and exploration are key to mastering these tools and unlocking the power of AI. The journey into AI is filled with challenges and discoveries; embrace the process, and celebrate your progress along the way.

Understanding the Jupyter Notebook Interface

Having successfully set up your Python environment and installed the necessary libraries, we now turn our attention to the Jupyter Notebook—your primary interface for interactive AI development. Jupyter Notebooks provide a powerful and user-friendly environment that seamlessly blends code execution, rich text documentation, and data visualization. This integrated approach makes it ideal for prototyping, experimenting, and documenting your AI projects. This section will guide you through the Jupyter Notebook interface, showing you how to navigate its features and leverage them for efficient AI development.

Let's start by launching Jupyter Notebook. If you installed Anaconda, simply open the Anaconda Navigator and click the launch button for Jupyter Notebook. Alternatively, you can open your terminal or command prompt and type `jupyter notebook` and press Enter. This will open a new tab in your web browser, displaying the Jupyter Notebook dashboard. This dashboard lists all the files and folders in your current directory. You can navigate through your file system using the interface just as you would in a typical file explorer. Creating a new notebook is straightforward; simply click the "New" button in the top right corner and select "Python 3" (or whichever Python kernel you've configured). This will open a new notebook, ready for your AI experimentation.

The Jupyter Notebook interface is organized into cells. Each cell can contain either code or Markdown text. Code cells are where you write and execute your Python code. Markdown cells allow you to add formatted text, headings, equations, images, and more, creating a rich documentation environment for your projects. This capability to combine code and explanatory text makes Jupyter Notebooks exceptionally effective for documenting the process of building and testing AI models, aiding in understanding and collaboration. The ability to blend code and narrative makes it incredibly powerful for teaching and learning.

Let's examine code cells first. Click on a code cell to select it. You'll notice that a green border highlights the active cell. Type some Python code, for instance, a simple print statement: `print("Hello, Jupyter!")`. To execute the code, press `Shift + Enter`. The code will run, and the output will appear below the cell. If your code produces a plot using Matplotlib, the plot will also be rendered directly within the notebook. This immediate feedback loop is what makes Jupyter Notebooks so conducive to interactive development. Experiment with various Python commands, such as arithmetic operations, variable assignments, and function calls—observe the immediate results and learn the language's behavior in a dynamic manner.

Now, let's explore Markdown cells. To create a new cell, click the "+" button in the toolbar above. Select "Markdown" from the dropdown menu that appears. You can now write formatted text using Markdown syntax. For example, to create a heading, use the `` ` `` symbol followed by your heading text. For instance, `` ` My AI Project` `` will render as a level 1 heading. `` ` Data Preprocessing` `` will render as a level 2 heading. Use `` ` ``
bold text
`` ` `` for bold text and `` ` ``
italics
`` ` `` for italicized text. You can add numbered and bulleted lists, insert images using the syntax `` `! ``
Image caption
`` ` ``, and even embed LaTeX equations using the dollar sign delimiters (`` `$...$` `` for inline equations and `` `$$...$$` `` for display
equations). The preview of these elements will be rendered directly in your notebook. Learning the basic Markdown

syntax is critical to making your notebooks readable and easy to share.

Beyond code execution and Markdown, Jupyter Notebooks offer a range of functionalities for efficient cell management. You can cut, copy, and paste cells, using the standard keyboard shortcuts or the toolbar buttons. You can also change the cell type between "Code" and "Markdown" using the dropdown menu in the toolbar. This flexibility allows you to rearrange and reorganize your work as needed. Moreover, you can add new cells above or below the currently selected cell. This is incredibly useful for iterative refinement and experimentation in your AI development process. As you develop your model, it's beneficial to experiment with different approaches, and this dynamic structure in Jupyter Notebooks allows you to easily add, test, and compare different ideas.

Let's work through a simple example incorporating both code and Markdown. Suppose we want to explore linear regression using NumPy and Matplotlib. First, create a Markdown cell and add a title: `Linear Regression Example`. Below this, create a code cell and import the necessary libraries:

```python
import numpy as np
import matplotlib.pyplot as plt
```

Next, generate some sample data:

```python
X = np.array([1, 2, 3, 4, 5])
y = np.array([2, 4, 5, 4, 5])
```

Now, let's perform a simple linear regression using NumPy's `polyfit` function. This function calculates the coefficients of a polynomial that best fits the data. In this case, we are fitting a line (a polynomial of degree 1):

```python
coefficients = np.polyfit(X, y, 1)
slope = coefficients[0]
intercept = coefficients[1]
```

We can then predict y values based on our model:

```python
y_predicted = slope X + intercept
```

Finally, let's visualize the results using Matplotlib:

```python
plt.scatter(X, y, label='Original Data')
plt.plot(X, y_predicted, color='red', label='Regression Line')
plt.xlabel('X')
plt.ylabel('y')
plt.title('Linear Regression')
plt.legend()
plt.show()
```

This example demonstrates the power of Jupyter Notebooks—combining code for data manipulation and model building with Markdown for clear explanations and visualization to provide a cohesive and understandable development process. Remember to save your notebook frequently to avoid losing your work. The `.ipynb` file format allows for saving both code and Markdown content, preserving the entire workflow.

Moving beyond this basic example, you can use Jupyter Notebooks to explore various aspects of AI development. You can load and preprocess datasets using Pandas, create and train complex neural networks using TensorFlow or PyTorch, and visualize the results using Matplotlib and other visualization libraries. The interactive nature of Jupyter Notebooks makes it an invaluable tool for experimenting with different algorithms, hyperparameters, and data preprocessing techniques. The ability to immediately see the results of your changes allows for rapid iterative development, crucial for efficient machine learning projects. As you progress through this book, you will extensively utilize Jupyter Notebooks to build and analyze various AI models.

Mastering the Jupyter Notebook interface is a cornerstone of your AI development journey. Its integrated approach to code, documentation, and visualization streamlines your workflow, enhances your understanding of the processes, and allows for a more efficient and effective learning experience. Therefore, familiarize yourself with its various functionalities, experiment with different features, and use it consistently throughout your exploration of the world of artificial intelligence. Remember, practice is key; the more you use Jupyter Notebooks, the more proficient you will become in leveraging its power for your AI projects. Through consistent usage, you'll quickly appreciate the efficiency and clarity it brings to your work. The ability to combine narrative explanations with executable code makes it an invaluable tool throughout your learning process. Consider it an essential part of your AI development toolkit, and you'll greatly enhance your ability to explore and understand AI concepts. The integration of code and explanation makes it an ideal platform for showcasing your work and collaborating with others.

Essential Data Structures in Python

Building robust and efficient AI systems hinges on your ability to effectively manage and manipulate data. Python, with its rich ecosystem of libraries and built-in data structures, provides the tools necessary for this task. While Python offers a range of data structures, mastering a few key ones forms the foundation for efficient AI programming. Let's delve into lists, dictionaries, and NumPy arrays, three fundamental data structures that are indispensable in the world of AI development.

Lists are perhaps the most intuitive data structure in Python. They are ordered, mutable sequences of items. This means you can change their contents after creation, and the order of elements is preserved. Lists can contain elements of different data types, including numbers, strings, and even other lists (creating nested lists). This flexibility makes them incredibly versatile for storing diverse datasets commonly encountered in AI.

For example, imagine you are working with a dataset of housing prices. Each house can be represented as a list containing features like square footage, number of bedrooms, number of bathrooms, and the price. Consider the following example:

```python
house1 = [1500, 3, 2, 300000] Square footage, bedrooms, bathrooms, price
house2 = [2000, 4, 3, 450000]
house3 = [1200, 2, 1, 250000]

houses = [house1, house2, house3] A list of houses
```

Here, `houses` is a list of lists, representing a simple dataset. You can access individual elements using indexing, starting from 0. For example, `houses[0]` accesses the first house (`house1`), and `houses[0][2]` accesses the number of bathrooms in the first house (which is 2). Lists also support various operations, including appending, inserting, removing, and sorting elements. These operations are crucial for data preprocessing and manipulation.

```python
houses.append([1800, 3, 2.5, 375000]) Adding a new house

houses.sort(key=lambda x: x[3]) Sorting houses by price
(ascending order). The lambda function specifies that the
sorting should be based on the 4th element (price).

print(houses)
```

The flexibility of lists makes them ideal for representing various datasets, but their lack of inherent structure can sometimes make data access and manipulation less efficient, particularly for very large datasets. This is where dictionaries come into play.

Dictionaries in Python are unordered collections of key-value pairs. Each key is unique and maps to a specific value. This structure makes dictionaries extremely efficient for looking up values based on keys. Think of a dictionary as a lookup table, offering $O(1)$ average-case time complexity for accessing elements. This is a significant advantage over lists, which have $O(n)$ time complexity for searching.

Returning to our housing price example, we can represent the data using a dictionary:

```python
house_data = {
'house1': {'sqft': 1500, 'bedrooms': 3, 'bathrooms': 2, 'price': 300000},
'house2': {'sqft': 2000, 'bedrooms': 4, 'bathrooms': 3, 'price': 450000},
'house3': {'sqft': 1200, 'bedrooms': 2, 'bathrooms': 1, 'price': 250000}
}

print(house_data['house1']['price']) Accessing the price of house1.
```

In this case, each house is a dictionary with keys representing features (e.g., 'sqft', 'bedrooms') and values representing their corresponding values. Accessing data becomes much more intuitive and readable compared to using nested lists.

Dictionaries are particularly beneficial in AI when working with feature vectors. Each key can represent a feature, and the corresponding value represents the feature's value for a given data point. This organized structure enhances readability and facilitates efficient data processing.

While lists and dictionaries are valuable, they fall short when dealing with numerical computations crucial in many AI tasks. This is where NumPy arrays shine.

NumPy (Numerical Python) is a powerful library that provides support for large, multi-dimensional arrays and matrices, along with a collection of high-level mathematical functions to operate on these arrays. NumPy arrays are significantly more efficient than Python lists for numerical operations, due to their homogeneous data type and optimized memory layout. They are the backbone of many AI and machine learning libraries, including TensorFlow and PyTorch.

Let's illustrate how NumPy arrays can be used with our housing data:

```python
import numpy as np

house_prices = np.array([300000, 450000, 250000, 375000])
house_sizes = np.array([1500, 2000, 1200, 1800])

average_price = np.mean(house_prices)
median_size = np.median(house_sizes)

print(f"Average price: {average_price}")
print(f"Median size: {median_size}")
```

This example demonstrates the efficiency of NumPy for performing numerical calculations. NumPy functions like `mean` and `median` are highly optimized, resulting in considerably faster computation compared to equivalent operations on Python lists.

Furthermore, NumPy supports vectorized operations, allowing you to perform operations on entire arrays without explicit loops. This significantly improves performance, especially when working with large datasets. For instance, you could calculate the average price per square foot by simply dividing the `house_prices` array by the `house_sizes` array:

```python
price_per_sqft = house_prices / house_sizes
print(price_per_sqft)
```

The ability to perform vectorized operations is a key advantage of NumPy arrays in AI programming. It not only improves code readability but also significantly speeds up computations, which is crucial when training complex AI models on large datasets.

Moreover, NumPy supports multi-dimensional arrays, making it ideal for representing images, which are fundamentally 2D arrays of pixel values. A color image, for instance, can be represented as a 3D array with dimensions (height, width, color channels). This capability extends to other higher-dimensional datasets commonly found in AI applications.

NumPy's efficiency stems from its use of contiguous memory allocation and its ability to leverage optimized C code for many of its operations. This contrast with Python lists, which are dynamically allocated and store pointers to objects of potentially varying types. The homogenous nature and contiguous memory allocation of NumPy arrays allow for efficient vectorization and optimized operations.

In essence, mastering lists, dictionaries, and NumPy arrays provides a solid foundation for your journey into AI programming. Lists provide flexibility for diverse data storage, dictionaries offer efficient key-based data access, and NumPy arrays provide the performance needed for numerical computations and handling multi-dimensional data. These data structures, combined with Python's versatile syntax and extensive libraries, equip you with the tools to effectively manage and manipulate the vast amounts of data inherent in AI development. Understanding their strengths and limitations, and knowing when to apply each, will prove invaluable as you progress through more complex AI concepts and projects. Remember that consistent practice with these fundamental data structures is key to developing proficiency and building intuition for data manipulation, a critical skill set in the field of artificial intelligence.

Introduction to Data Manipulation with Pandas

Building upon our foundational understanding of Python's core data structures, we now introduce Pandas, a powerful Python library specifically designed for data manipulation and analysis. Pandas is an indispensable tool in the AI development workflow, providing efficient methods for cleaning, transforming, and preparing data for use in machine learning models. At its core lies the DataFrame, a two-dimensional labeled data structure with columns of potentially different types. Think of it as a highly organized and flexible spreadsheet, far exceeding the capabilities of a simple spreadsheet program.

Let's begin with the basics of creating and manipulating Pandas DataFrames. The most common way to create a DataFrame is from a dictionary. Suppose we have data representing the sales figures for different products over a few months:

```python
import pandas as pd

data = {'Product': ['A', 'B', 'C', 'A', 'B', 'C'],
'Month': ['January', 'January', 'January', 'February', 'February', 'February'],
'Sales': [100, 150, 200, 120, 180, 220]}

df = pd.DataFrame(data)
print(df)
```

This code snippet creates a DataFrame named `df` containing three columns: 'Product', 'Month', and 'Sales'.

Pandas automatically infers the data types of each column. Printing the DataFrame displays its contents in a tabular format, making it easily readable. You can access individual columns using bracket notation:

```python
print(df['Product'])
```

This will print the 'Product' column. You can also access multiple columns by passing a list of column names:

```python
print(df[['Product', 'Sales']])
```

This prints the 'Product' and 'Sales' columns. DataFrames are not limited to simple numerical and string data; they can handle a wide variety of data types, including dates, times, and even more complex custom objects.

One of the most crucial aspects of data manipulation is data cleaning. Real-world datasets are rarely perfect; they often contain missing values, inconsistencies, and errors. Pandas provides tools to handle these issues effectively. Missing values are often represented as `NaN` (Not a Number). We can identify and count missing values using:

```python
print(df.isnull().sum())
```

This will give us the count of missing values in each column. We can handle missing values in several ways. A common approach is to fill them with a suitable value, such as the mean, median, or a specific constant. For example, to fill missing values in the 'Sales' column with the mean:

```python
df['Sales'].fillna(df['Sales'].mean(), inplace=True)
```

`inplace=True` modifies the DataFrame directly; otherwise, a copy would be returned. Alternatively, we can remove rows with missing values entirely:

```python
df.dropna(inplace=True)
```

This is a more drastic approach, and should only be used if removing the rows doesn't significantly bias your data. Careful consideration of the implications of missing data handling is crucial for accurate AI model training.

Data filtering allows us to select specific subsets of the data based on certain conditions. For example, to select only the rows where the 'Sales' are greater than 170:

```python
filtered_df = df[df['Sales'] > 170]
print(filtered_df)
```

This creates a new DataFrame `filtered_df` containing only the rows that meet the condition. Multiple conditions can be combined using logical operators like `&` (and) and `|` (or):

```python
filtered_df = df[(df['Sales'] > 170) & (df['Product'] == 'B')]
print(filtered_df)
```

This selects rows where 'Sales' is greater than 170 AND the 'Product' is 'B'. This precise control over data selection is essential for creating focused datasets tailored to specific AI model training needs.

Data transformation is another critical aspect of data preparation. This involves modifying the existing data to create new features or to improve the data's suitability for modeling. For example, we can create a new column representing the sales per unit if we have a "Units Sold" column. Let's add a hypothetical "Units Sold" column:

```python
df['Units Sold'] = [10, 15, 20, 12, 18, 22]
df['Sales per Unit'] = df['Sales'] / df['Units Sold']
print(df)
```

This demonstrates creating a new column ('Sales per Unit') based on calculations involving existing columns. Another common transformation is converting categorical variables into numerical representations, which is often necessary for many machine learning algorithms. Pandas provides the `get_dummies()` function for this purpose:

```python
pd.get_dummies(df['Product'])
```

This converts the categorical 'Product' column into multiple binary columns, one for each unique product. These transformed columns can then be included in the dataset used for training your AI models. Further transformations might involve scaling or normalizing numerical features to improve model performance and prevent features with larger values from dominating the model.

Let's consider a more complex example, involving data cleaning and transformation. Imagine we have a dataset with customer information containing missing values and inconsistent data formatting:

```python
customer_data = {'CustomerID': [1, 2, 3, 4, 5],
'Name': ['Alice', 'Bob', 'Charlie', 'Dave', 'Eve'],
'Age': [25, 30, None, 35, 40],
'City': ['New York', 'London', 'London', 'Paris', 'New York'],
'PurchaseAmount': ['$100', '$150', '$200', '$120', '180']}

customer df = pd.DataFrame(customer data)
print(customer_df)
```

First, let's handle the missing age. We'll fill it with the median age:

```python
customer df['Age'].fillna(customer df['Age'].median(), inplace=True)
```

Next, the 'PurchaseAmount' column contains inconsistencies— some values have dollar signs. Let's clean this column:

```python
customer df['PurchaseAmount'] = customer df['PurchaseAmount'].astype(str).str.replace(r'[$,]', '', regex=True).astype(float)
```

This line of code first converts the column to strings, removes dollar signs and commas using regular expressions, then converts back to floating-point numbers. We might then want to create additional features, such as a boolean column indicating whether the customer lives in London:

```python
customer
df['LondonCustomer'] = customer
df['City'] == 'London'
print(customer_df)
```

These data cleaning and transformation steps demonstrate a typical preprocessing pipeline for preparing real-world data for AI model training. The careful handling of missing data, inconsistent data formats and the creation of new informative features is a critical part of building accurate and effective AI systems. Pandas provides an exceptionally convenient way to manage these essential aspects of AI development. Remember that the specific cleaning and transformation steps will depend heavily on the nature of your data and the requirements of your AI model. Thorough exploration and understanding of your data are always the first steps.

Finally, Pandas offers efficient tools for data aggregation and summarization. For instance, we can calculate the average sales per product:

```python
print(df.groupby('Product')['Sales'].mean())
```

This groups the data by product and calculates the mean sales for each group. Similar aggregations can be performed for other statistical measures, providing valuable insights into your data. This ability to efficiently summarize and understand data trends is crucial for data exploration and for making informed decisions during the AI model development process. The power and flexibility of Pandas make it an invaluable tool in every stage of the AI development lifecycle. Mastering Pandas is a significant step towards building robust and effective AI solutions.

Data Visualization with Matplotlib

Having established a robust foundation in data manipulation with Pandas, we now turn our attention to data visualization—a critical aspect of the AI development process. Effective visualization allows us to explore data, identify patterns, understand model performance, and communicate insights effectively. Matplotlib, a powerful and versatile Python library, is our tool of choice for this task. It provides a comprehensive set of functions for creating static, interactive, and animated visualizations in various formats.

Matplotlib's strength lies in its flexibility. While it offers a straightforward interface for creating basic plots, its extensive capabilities allow for the customization of virtually every aspect of a visualization, enabling the creation of publication-quality figures tailored to specific needs. This adaptability is crucial in AI, where the complexity of data and models often demands nuanced visual representations.

Let's begin with the simplest plot: the line plot. This is ideal for showcasing trends over time or across a continuous variable. Consider a scenario where we're monitoring the accuracy of a machine learning model during training. We can use Matplotlib to plot the accuracy against the number of training epochs. This visual representation immediately highlights whether the model is learning effectively, if it's converging to a solution, or if it's experiencing overfitting or underfitting.

```python
import matplotlib.pyplot as plt
import numpy as np
```

Sample data representing model accuracy over epochs

```
epochs = np.arange(1, 101)
accuracy = 0.8 + 0.1 * np.sin(epochs / 10) + 0.05 * np.random.randn(100)

plt.plot(epochs, accuracy)
plt.xlabel("Epoch")
plt.ylabel("Accuracy")
plt.title("Model Accuracy During Training")
plt.grid(True)
plt.show()
```

This code snippet generates a simple line plot showcasing the accuracy over 100 epochs. The `plt.xlabel`, `plt.ylabel`, and `plt.title` functions add descriptive labels to the axes and the plot itself, enhancing readability. `plt.grid(True)` adds a grid to the plot, making it easier to read values. The `plt.show()` function finally displays the generated plot. Notice the use of NumPy to generate sample data for demonstration purposes; in a real-world scenario, this data would come from your model's training logs.

Beyond line plots, Matplotlib excels in creating scatter plots, histograms, bar charts, and many other visualization types. Scatter plots are invaluable for visualizing relationships between two variables. For example, we might use a scatter plot to explore the correlation between two features in a dataset, identifying potential linear or non-linear relationships.

```python
```

Sample data representing two features

```
feature1 = np.random.rand(100)
feature2 = 2 * feature1 + 0.5 * np.random.randn(100)

plt.scatter(feature1, feature2)
plt.xlabel("Feature 1")
plt.ylabel("Feature 2")
plt.title("Scatter Plot of Two Features")
plt.show()
```

This code generates a scatter plot showcasing the relationship between `feature1` and `feature2`. The correlation between the features is immediately apparent from the visual representation. This is a far more intuitive way to understand the relationship than simply examining numerical correlation coefficients.

Histograms are crucial for visualizing the distribution of a single variable. They provide insights into the central tendency, spread, and skewness of the data. In AI, histograms are useful for understanding the distribution of features, identifying outliers, and assessing the effectiveness of data preprocessing techniques.

```python
```

Sample data representing a single feature

```
data = np.random.randn(1000)

plt.hist(data, bins=30)
plt.xlabel("Feature Value")
plt.ylabel("Frequency")
plt.title("Histogram of Feature Distribution")
plt.show()
```

This code generates a histogram with 30 bins, illustrating the distribution of the `data` variable. The choice of the number of bins influences the visual representation, and it's often beneficial to experiment with different bin counts to find the most informative visualization.

Bar charts are particularly effective for comparing categorical data. For example, we might use a bar chart to show the performance of different machine learning models on a specific dataset, comparing metrics like accuracy, precision, and recall.

```python
```

Sample data representing model performance

```
models = ['Model A', 'Model B', 'Model C']
accuracy = [0.85, 0.92, 0.78]

plt.bar(models, accuracy)
plt.xlabel("Model")
plt.ylabel("Accuracy")
plt.title("Model Accuracy Comparison")
plt.show()
```

This code generates a simple bar chart comparing the accuracy of three different models. The clear visual comparison makes it easy to identify the best-performing model.

Matplotlib also supports more advanced plotting techniques such as creating subplots, which allow you to arrange multiple plots within a single figure, improving the overall clarity and efficiency of your visualizations. This is particularly useful when you need to present multiple aspects of your data or model performance simultaneously. For instance, you could create a figure with a line plot showing training accuracy, a histogram showing the distribution of a key feature, and a scatter plot showing the relationship between two features – all within a single, well-organized visualization.

Furthermore, Matplotlib allows for extensive customization. You can change colors, line styles, marker shapes, add legends, annotations, and much more. This granular control allows you to create visualizations that are not only informative but also visually appealing and easy to interpret. Experimenting with different styles and aesthetics can significantly enhance the impact of your visualizations.

Beyond static plots, Matplotlib can also be used to create interactive plots, allowing users to zoom, pan, and explore the data more dynamically. While this often requires integration with other libraries or tools, the underlying plotting capabilities provided by Matplotlib form the foundation for these interactive experiences.

In summary, Matplotlib is an indispensable tool in any AI developer's arsenal. Its versatility, ease of use, and extensive customization options make it the perfect choice for visualizing data distributions, exploring relationships between variables, monitoring model performance, and effectively communicating insights. Mastering Matplotlib is a crucial step in developing a deep understanding of your data and your AI models. The examples provided here offer just a glimpse of its capabilities; thorough exploration of Matplotlib's documentation and experimentation with different plotting techniques are highly encouraged. The ability to visualize data effectively is a significant advantage in the field of AI, enabling better decision-making and faster progress in developing robust and accurate AI systems. The time invested in learning Matplotlib will be repaid many times over in increased efficiency and deeper understanding throughout your AI journey. From simple line graphs to complex multi-plot figures, Matplotlib provides the tools you need to visually interpret and communicate the results of your work. Remember to experiment with different plot types, styles, and customizations to find the most effective ways to represent your data and insights. Effective data visualization is not simply about presenting data; it's about uncovering patterns, making discoveries, and communicating your findings effectively to others.

Supervised Learning Concepts

Supervised learning forms the cornerstone of many machine learning applications. At its heart, it's a learning paradigm where an algorithm learns to map inputs to outputs based on a labeled dataset. This dataset consists of pairs of input features and their corresponding target values or labels. The algorithm's goal is to learn a function that can accurately predict the output for unseen inputs. Think of it like a teacher supervising a student's learning process – the teacher provides examples (the labeled dataset), and the student (the algorithm) learns to generalize from these examples to solve new problems.

The process begins with a dataset containing features (the characteristics of the data points) and labels (the correct outputs). For example, in image classification, the features might be the pixel values of an image, and the labels would be the category the image belongs to (e.g., "cat," "dog," "bird"). The algorithm analyzes this dataset, identifying patterns and relationships between the features and labels. This learned relationship is then encoded within a model, which can be used to make predictions on new, unseen data.

There are two main branches of supervised learning: regression and classification. Regression deals with predicting a continuous output variable, while classification focuses on predicting a categorical output variable.

Regression:
In regression problems, the target variable is continuous. This means it can take on any value within a certain range. Consider predicting house prices based on features like size, location, and number of bedrooms. The house price is a continuous variable, as it can be any value

within a reasonable range (e.g., $200,000, $250,500, $317,890). Common regression algorithms include linear regression, polynomial regression, support vector regression (SVR), and decision tree regression. Linear regression, for instance, models the relationship between the input features and the output variable using a linear equation. More complex algorithms like SVR can handle non-linear relationships.

Let's illustrate with a simple example. Imagine we want to predict a student's final exam score based on their midterm score. We collect data from past students, pairing their midterm scores (input feature) with their final exam scores (output variable). We can then use linear regression to find the best-fitting line through these data points. This line represents the learned function that maps midterm scores to predicted final exam scores. Given a new student's midterm score, we can use this line to estimate their expected final exam score. The equation of the line would be of the form: `Final Exam Score = m Midterm Score + c`, where 'm' is the slope and 'c' is the y-intercept, determined by the algorithm during training.

Classification:
In classification problems, the target variable is categorical. This means it can only take on a finite set of values. Examples include image classification (cat, dog, bird), spam detection (spam, not spam), and medical diagnosis (cancer, no cancer). Popular classification algorithms include logistic regression, support vector machines (SVMs), decision trees, and naive Bayes. Logistic regression, for instance, models the probability of an input belonging to a particular category. Support vector machines aim to find the optimal hyperplane that separates different categories in the feature space.

Consider the task of classifying emails as spam or not spam. We can use features like the presence of certain words ("free," "money," "prize"), the length of the email, and the sender's email address. A classification algorithm, such as logistic regression, would learn to map these features to the labels "spam" or "not spam." Given a new email, the algorithm would use the learned model to predict whether it's spam or not. The output would be a probability score indicating the likelihood of the email being spam. A threshold (e.g., 0.5) would then be applied to classify the email as spam or not spam.

Choosing the Right Algorithm:
The choice of algorithm depends on several factors, including the nature of the data (e.g., linear vs. non-linear relationships), the size of the dataset, and the computational resources available. Simple algorithms like linear regression and logistic regression are computationally efficient and work well for linearly
separable data. More complex algorithms like support vector machines and decision trees can handle non-linear relationships but may require more computational power.

Model Training and Evaluation:
Training a supervised learning model involves feeding the labeled dataset to the algorithm. The algorithm adjusts its internal parameters to minimize the difference between its predictions and the actual labels in the training data. This process is often iterative, with the algorithm making adjustments in each iteration to improve its accuracy.

Once the model is trained, it needs to be evaluated to assess its performance on unseen data. This is done using a separate dataset called the test set, which was not used during training. Common evaluation metrics for regression include mean squared error (MSE) and R-squared, while for classification, metrics like accuracy, precision, recall, F1-

score, and area under the ROC curve (AUC) are commonly used. These metrics provide quantitative measures of the model's performance and help determine its suitability for the specific application.

Overfitting and Underfitting:
A critical challenge in supervised learning is avoiding overfitting and underfitting. Overfitting occurs when the model learns the training data too well, including its noise, leading to poor generalization to unseen data. Underfitting occurs when the model is too simple to capture the underlying patterns in the data,
resulting in poor performance on both training and test data. Techniques like cross-validation, regularization (L1 and L2 regularization), and early stopping can help mitigate overfitting. Feature selection and engineering play a significant role in improving model performance by selecting the most relevant features and transforming them into a form that is more suitable for the learning algorithm. Careful selection and pre-processing of features can significantly improve model accuracy and robustness. This often involves techniques like dimensionality reduction (PCA) to reduce the number of features and remove redundant information.

Supervised learning is a powerful tool with a wide range of applications in various fields, including image recognition, natural language processing, medical diagnosis, fraud detection, and many more. Understanding the fundamental concepts, algorithms, and evaluation metrics is crucial for anyone looking to build and deploy successful machine learning models. The ability to choose the appropriate algorithm, effectively train the model, and evaluate its performance is paramount for building robust and reliable AI systems. By mastering the nuances of supervised learning, you will equip yourselves with a foundational skillset that will serve as a building block for more advanced machine learning techniques and applications discussed in the following chapters.

Unsupervised Learning Techniques

Unsupervised learning represents a significant departure from the supervised learning paradigm we've just explored. Instead of relying on labeled data, where each data point is explicitly tagged with its corresponding class or target value, unsupervised learning operates on unlabeled data. This means the algorithm must discern patterns, structures, and relationships within the data without any prior knowledge of the correct answers. This inherent challenge necessitates a different set of algorithms and techniques, focusing on uncovering inherent characteristics within the data itself. The power of unsupervised learning lies in its ability to discover hidden insights and structures that might be missed by human observation or traditional data analysis methods. This section will delve into some fundamental unsupervised learning techniques, highlighting their strengths, weaknesses, and practical applications.

One of the most prevalent unsupervised learning tasks is **clustering**, which aims to group similar data points together. Imagine having a large dataset of customer purchase histories. Clustering algorithms could help segment these customers into distinct groups based on their purchasing behaviors, allowing for targeted marketing campaigns or personalized product recommendations. A widely used clustering algorithm is **K-means**, a relatively simple yet effective method. K-means works by iteratively assigning data points to the nearest cluster centroid, recalculating the centroids based on the assigned points, and repeating this process until the cluster assignments stabilize. The "K" in K-means refers to the predefined number of clusters, which is often determined through experimentation or by using techniques like the elbow method, which plots the within-cluster sum of squares against the number of clusters. The elbow point on the resulting plot suggests an optimal number of clusters.

However, the choice of 'K' is a crucial parameter and directly influences the outcome of the K-means algorithm. An inappropriately chosen 'K' can lead to inaccurate or meaningless clusters. Moreover, K-means is sensitive to the initial placement of centroids and can sometimes converge to local optima, rather than the global optimum clustering. This limitation can be mitigated by running the algorithm multiple times with different initializations and choosing the solution with the lowest within-cluster sum of squares.

Beyond K-means, a plethora of other clustering algorithms exist, each with its strengths and weaknesses.
Hierarchical clustering
, for example, builds a hierarchy of clusters, either agglomeratively (bottom-up) or divisively (top-down). Agglomerative clustering starts with each data point as a separate cluster and iteratively merges the closest clusters until a single cluster remains. Divisive clustering, conversely, begins with a single cluster and recursively divides it into smaller clusters. The resulting dendrogram visually represents the hierarchical relationships between clusters, allowing for a deeper understanding of the data's structure. However, hierarchical clustering can be computationally expensive for large datasets.

Another important class of unsupervised learning techniques involves
dimensionality reduction
. High-dimensional data, often encountered in fields like image processing and
genomics, poses challenges for both computational efficiency and model interpretability. Dimensionality reduction techniques aim to reduce the number of variables while preserving as much relevant information as possible. This is achieved by projecting the data onto a lower-

dimensional subspace. One of the most widely used dimensionality reduction methods is **Principal Component Analysis (PCA)**. PCA identifies the principal components, which are orthogonal directions that capture the maximum variance in the data. By projecting the data onto the first few principal components, we can effectively reduce the dimensionality while retaining most of the important information.

PCA relies on the covariance matrix of the data to find the principal components. The eigenvectors of this matrix correspond to the principal components, and their eigenvalues represent the amount of variance explained by each component. The selection of the number of principal components to retain is crucial. This decision is often guided by the cumulative explained variance. We typically choose the number of components that explains a sufficient percentage (e.g., 95%) of the total variance. The benefit of this dimensionality reduction is not only a decrease in computational cost but also improved model interpretability and noise reduction. In high-dimensional data, noise can often mask true patterns. PCA aids in noise reduction by focusing on the directions of maximal variance, effectively filtering out less significant variations.

However, PCA assumes linearity in the data. If the underlying relationships within the data are non-linear, PCA might not be the optimal choice. In such cases, non-linear dimensionality reduction techniques, like **t-distributed Stochastic Neighbor Embedding (t-SNE)**, become more appropriate. t-SNE excels at visualizing high-dimensional data in a lower-dimensional space, often two or three dimensions, revealing underlying clusters and relationships that might be invisible in the original data. While t-SNE is excellent for visualization, it's computationally intensive and its results can be sensitive to the choice of parameters.

Beyond clustering and dimensionality reduction, unsupervised learning encompasses other crucial techniques such as **anomaly detection**, which aims to identify unusual or outlier data points that deviate significantly from the norm. This is invaluable in fraud detection, network security, and manufacturing quality control. Algorithms like **One-Class SVM** and **isolation forest** are commonly employed for anomaly detection. One-Class SVM builds a model representing the "normal" data, and points outside this model are flagged as anomalies. The isolation forest algorithm isolates anomalies by randomly partitioning the data, with the assumption that anomalies require fewer partitions to isolate.

Furthermore, **association rule mining** is another significant unsupervised learning technique used to discover relationships between variables in large datasets. This is often used in market basket analysis, identifying items frequently purchased together. The Apriori algorithm is a popular method for association rule mining, identifying frequent itemsets and then generating association rules based on support and confidence metrics. Support measures how frequently an itemset appears in the dataset, while confidence indicates the probability that one itemset will appear given the presence of another. This technique is widely employed in retail to optimize product placement and improve targeted marketing strategies.

In conclusion, unsupervised learning provides a powerful toolkit for exploring and understanding unlabeled data. The techniques discussed in this section—clustering, dimensionality reduction, anomaly detection, and association rule mining—represent only a fraction of the available methods. The choice of the appropriate technique depends heavily on the specific characteristics of the data and the goals of the analysis. Mastering these techniques is crucial for gaining valuable insights from data, enabling data-driven decision-making, and developing more robust and effective AI systems. The ability to identify hidden patterns and structures in data is invaluable across numerous domains, from business intelligence and scientific research to healthcare and finance, highlighting the broad impact and importance of unsupervised learning. The application of these techniques requires a deep understanding of the underlying algorithms and a careful consideration of the limitations and assumptions inherent in each method. The next chapter will expand upon these foundations and introduce the exciting world of reinforcement learning.

Model Evaluation Metrics

Having established the foundational concepts of supervised and unsupervised learning, we now transition to a crucial aspect of any machine learning project: model evaluation. No matter how elegantly designed or computationally intensive a model might be, its true worth is determined by its ability to accurately predict or classify unseen data. This section delves into the key metrics used to assess model performance, providing a clear understanding of their strengths and limitations. These metrics are indispensable tools for comparing different models, identifying areas for improvement, and ultimately building more reliable and robust AI systems.

The first and perhaps most intuitive metric is **accuracy**. Accuracy simply represents the ratio of correctly classified instances to the total number of instances. While seemingly straightforward, accuracy can be misleading, particularly in imbalanced datasets. Consider a medical diagnosis scenario where a rare disease affects only 1% of the population. A model that always predicts "no disease" will achieve 99% accuracy, yet it's utterly useless for detecting the disease. This highlights the limitations of accuracy when class distributions are skewed. In such cases, other metrics offer a more nuanced evaluation.

Let's delve into the concepts of **precision** and **recall**, two metrics that provide a more granular view of model performance, particularly in imbalanced datasets. Precision answers the question: "Of all the instances predicted as positive, what proportion was actually positive?" In simpler terms, it measures the accuracy of positive predictions. A high precision score indicates that when the model predicts a positive outcome, it's largely correct.

Recall, on the other hand, addresses a different aspect: "Of all the instances that are actually positive, what proportion did the model correctly identify?" Recall focuses on the model's ability to capture all the true positive instances. A high recall score suggests that the model is effectively identifying most of the positive instances, even if it might make some false positive predictions as well.

The relationship between precision and recall often involves a trade-off. Increasing precision might decrease recall, and vice versa. This trade-off is crucial to consider in various applications. For instance, in spam detection, high recall is prioritized to minimize missing actual spam emails, even if it means accepting some false positives (legitimate emails classified as spam). Conversely, in medical diagnosis, high precision is often favored to minimize false positives (incorrect diagnoses), even if it results in missing some true positive cases.

To combine the insights offered by precision and recall, the **F1-score**
is employed. The F1-score is the harmonic mean of precision and recall, providing a single metric that balances both. This is particularly useful when there's a need for a balanced measure of both precision and recall, avoiding the biases that may arise from focusing on one metric alone. A high F1-score indicates a good balance between minimizing false positives and false negatives.

The choice between using precision, recall, or the F1-score depends heavily on the specific application. In cases where false positives are significantly more costly than false negatives (e.g., medical diagnosis), precision might be prioritized. Conversely, if the cost of false negatives outweighs false positives (e.g., spam detection), recall takes precedence. The F1-score provides a balanced perspective when neither false positive nor false negative carries significantly higher weight.

Beyond precision, recall, and the F1-score, the **Area Under the ROC Curve (AUC)** provides a valuable measure of model performance, especially for binary classification problems. The ROC curve plots the true positive rate (recall) against the false positive rate (the proportion of negative instances incorrectly classified as positive) at various classification thresholds. The AUC represents the area under this curve. An AUC of 1 indicates a perfect classifier, while an AUC of 0.5 indicates a random classifier. Generally, a higher AUC signifies better model performance. AUC is particularly useful when dealing with imbalanced datasets because it's less sensitive to class distribution compared to accuracy.

The interpretation of these metrics requires careful consideration of the context. For example, an AUC of 0.9 might be considered excellent in one application but merely acceptable in another, depending on the specific requirements and the baseline performance of other models. It's also crucial to understand the limitations of these metrics. They provide a snapshot of a model's performance on a specific dataset and might not generalize perfectly to other datasets or real-world scenarios.

Let's illustrate these concepts with an example. Suppose we're building a model to detect fraudulent credit card transactions. A high recall is crucial here to minimize missing fraudulent transactions, even if it leads to some false positives (legitimate transactions flagged as fraudulent). A low recall would mean many fraudulent transactions go undetected, leading to significant financial losses. However, excessively high recall could lead to a large number of legitimate transactions being blocked, causing inconvenience to customers. Therefore, a careful balance between recall and precision, possibly using the F1-score, is necessary. The AUC would further quantify the model's overall performance, indicating how well it discriminates between fraudulent and legitimate transactions.

Another illustrative example could be a spam filter. A high precision is desirable to minimize the number of legitimate emails being classified as spam (false positives), even if it means some spam emails might slip through (false negatives). While missing some spam is inconvenient, misclassifying legitimate emails can lead to lost business opportunities or important messages being overlooked. In such scenarios, precision often takes precedence over recall, though the F1-score provides a balanced perspective.

Furthermore, we must acknowledge that model evaluation is not a one-size-fits-all process. The appropriate metrics and evaluation techniques depend heavily on the specific problem, the nature of the data, and the cost associated with different types of errors. A thorough evaluation process requires considering a variety of metrics, along with domain expertise, to gain a comprehensive understanding of a model's strengths and weaknesses. It is crucial to avoid over-reliance on a single metric, as a high score on one metric may not necessarily reflect overall good performance.

In conclusion, the metrics discussed—accuracy, precision, recall, F1-score, and AUC—are invaluable tools in the arsenal of any machine learning practitioner. Their proper understanding and application are fundamental to developing reliable and effective AI systems. By carefully selecting the most appropriate metrics and interpreting the results within their context, we can ensure that our models not only perform well on test data but also generalize effectively to new, unseen data, ultimately contributing to the successful deployment and impact of our AI solutions. The ability to critically evaluate model performance is a hallmark of a skilled machine learning engineer, and these metrics form the bedrock of this essential skill. As we progress to more advanced model architectures and learning paradigms in later chapters, the importance of rigorous evaluation will only become more pronounced. Continuous monitoring and evaluation of model performance are essential for long-term success in any AI project. The choice of metric should always be informed by the specific application and the relative costs of different types of errors, ensuring that the evaluation process directly reflects the objectives of the AI system.

BiasVariance Tradeoff

Building upon our understanding of model evaluation metrics, we now turn our attention to a fundamental challenge in machine learning: the bias-variance tradeoff. This concept lies at the heart of understanding why some models generalize well to unseen data while others fail spectacularly. Essentially, the bias-variance tradeoff describes the tension between a model's ability to fit the training data (low bias) and its ability to generalize to new, unseen data (low variance). A model that is too complex can overfit the training data, capturing noise and idiosyncrasies specific to that dataset, leading to poor generalization. Conversely, a model that is too simple can underfit the data, failing to capture the underlying patterns and resulting in poor performance on both training and test sets.

Let's illustrate this with an analogy. Imagine you're trying to fit a curve to a set of scattered data points. A simple linear model (a straight line) might underfit the data, failing to capture the curvature present in the points. This results in high bias—the model's assumptions are too simplistic to accurately represent the data. On the other hand, a highly complex polynomial model, with many twists and turns, could overfit the data, following every single point closely, including the noise. This leads to high variance—the model is highly sensitive to the specific training data and would likely perform poorly on new data that doesn't perfectly match the training set's idiosyncrasies. The optimal model would strike a balance, capturing the underlying trend without being overly influenced by random noise.

Mathematically, we can decompose the expected squared error of a prediction into bias and variance components. The expected squared error measures the average difference between the model's predictions and the true values. High bias implies the model's average prediction is far from the true value, even if the predictions are consistent across different training sets. High variance, on the other hand, implies that the model's predictions vary greatly depending on the specific training data used. The ideal scenario is to minimize both bias and variance simultaneously.

Overfitting occurs when a model learns the training data too well, including its noise. This results in excellent performance on the training set but poor performance on unseen data. Think of a student who memorizes the answers to a practice test but struggles with the actual exam, which contains different questions. The student has overfit the practice test. In machine learning, overfitting manifests as a model that performs exceptionally well on the training data but poorly on the validation or test data. This is often indicated by a large gap between the training and testing error. Several factors contribute to overfitting, including overly complex models with too many parameters, insufficient training data, or noisy data.

Underfitting, conversely, happens when a model is too simple to capture the underlying patterns in the data. This results in poor performance on both training and test sets. In our curve-fitting analogy, the linear model underfits the data because it's too simplistic to capture the curvature. Similarly, using a linear regression model to predict complex non-linear relationships will inevitably lead to underfitting. The model simply lacks the capacity to represent the complexities of the data. The symptoms of underfitting include high error rates on both training and test data, and little to no improvement in performance as the model's complexity is increased.

To mitigate overfitting and underfitting, various regularization techniques are employed. Regularization adds constraints to the model's learning process, discouraging overly complex solutions. One common approach is L1 regularization (LASSO), which adds a penalty term proportional to the absolute value of the model's weights. This encourages sparsity, meaning that some weights are driven to zero, effectively simplifying the model. Another popular technique is L2 regularization (Ridge), which adds a penalty term proportional to the square of the model's weights. This shrinks the weights towards zero, reducing the model's complexity but without necessarily driving any weights to exactly zero. The choice between L1 and L2 regularization depends on the specific problem and the nature of the data.

Elastic Net regularization combines both L1 and L2 penalties, offering the benefits of both sparsity and weight shrinkage. This can be particularly useful when dealing with highly correlated features. Regularization parameters, such as the strength of the L1 or L2 penalty, are often tuned using techniques like cross-validation to find the optimal balance between model complexity and generalization performance.

Cross-validation is a powerful technique for evaluating model performance and tuning hyperparameters. It involves splitting the dataset into multiple folds, training the model on some folds, and validating it on the remaining fold(s). This process is repeated multiple times, with different folds used for training and validation, providing a more robust estimate of the model's performance than a simple train-test split. The most common type of cross-validation is k-fold cross-validation, where the data is divided into k equal-sized folds.

In k-fold cross-validation, the model is trained k times, each time using k-1 folds for training and one fold for validation.

The average performance across all k folds provides a more reliable measure of the model's generalization ability. This is particularly useful for smaller datasets, where a simple train-test split might lead to unreliable estimates of model performance due to the limited size of the test set. Cross-validation not only helps assess model performance but also allows for effective hyperparameter tuning. By performing cross-validation for different hyperparameter settings, we can select the setting that yields the best average performance across the folds.

Another important aspect of managing the bias-variance tradeoff is careful feature engineering. Selecting relevant features and creating effective features can significantly improve model performance and reduce both bias and variance. Irrelevant or redundant features can introduce noise and lead to overfitting. Therefore, feature selection and engineering are crucial steps in any machine learning project. Dimensionality reduction techniques, such as principal component analysis (PCA), can also help reduce the number of features, simplifying the model and preventing overfitting.

Furthermore, the size of the training dataset plays a crucial role in the bias-variance tradeoff. Larger datasets generally lead to better generalization, as they provide a more comprehensive representation of the underlying data distribution. With more data, the model is less likely to overfit to the idiosyncrasies of a limited sample. However, collecting and preparing large datasets can be challenging and expensive. Therefore, striking a balance between data size and the computational cost of training is often necessary.

In conclusion, the bias-variance tradeoff is a central challenge in machine learning. Understanding this tradeoff is critical for building effective and robust models. By employing techniques such as regularization, cross-validation, careful feature engineering, and using sufficiently large datasets, we can strive to minimize both bias and variance, creating models that generalize well to unseen data and effectively solve the problem at hand. The choice of techniques and the optimal balance between bias and variance will depend heavily on the specific context of the problem, the available data, and the computational resources at our disposal. Continuous experimentation and iterative model refinement are key to mastering this fundamental aspect of machine learning. The ongoing evolution of machine learning algorithms and techniques continues to refine our ability to navigate the bias-variance tradeoff, leading to increasingly sophisticated and reliable AI systems.

Feature Engineering and Selection

The success of any machine learning model hinges critically on the quality of the data it is trained on. While algorithms are undoubtedly important, the raw data, and how it's prepared, often plays a more significant role in determining the final performance. This is where feature engineering and selection come into play. These are not mere afterthoughts; they are crucial steps that can dramatically improve model accuracy, efficiency, and interpretability. Let's delve into these essential techniques.

Feature engineering is the process of using domain knowledge to extract features from raw data that make machine learning algorithms work better. It's a creative and iterative process, often requiring experimentation and a deep understanding of the problem domain. A well-engineered feature can capture important patterns and relationships in the data, leading to more accurate and robust models. Poorly engineered features, on the other hand, can lead to models that perform poorly or fail completely.

Consider a simple example: predicting house prices. Raw data might include the house's address, square footage, number of bedrooms, and year built. However, these raw features might not be sufficient. Effective feature engineering could involve creating new features such as: "price per square foot," "age of the house," "distance to the nearest school," or even more sophisticated features capturing neighborhood characteristics based on external data sources like crime rates or school rankings. These derived features often have a far stronger correlation with the target variable (house price) than the raw features. The act of creating these new features requires understanding what factors actually influence house prices.

The process often involves several key steps. First, we need a deep understanding of the data and the problem we're trying to solve. This may require talking to domain experts, conducting thorough exploratory data analysis (EDA), and visualizing the data. EDA helps in identifying potential relationships and patterns within the data which can inspire new features. For example, a scatter plot might reveal a non-linear relationship between two variables, suggesting a need for transforming one or both variables.

Next comes the transformation of existing features. This involves applying mathematical or statistical techniques to improve the quality and relevance of the features. Common transformations include:

Scaling:
Techniques like standardization (z-score normalization) or min-max scaling transform features to a specific range, preventing features with larger values from dominating the model. This is particularly important for algorithms sensitive to feature scaling, such as k-Nearest Neighbors (k-NN) and Support Vector Machines (SVMs).

Normalization:
This brings features to a similar scale, typically between 0 and 1. This can improve the performance of models that are sensitive to the scale of features, such as gradient descent-based algorithms.

Log transformation:
This is useful for handling skewed data, where a significant portion of the values is concentrated in a small range, and the rest are spread out over a large range. It compresses the range of high values and expands the range of low values, making the data more normally distributed.

One-hot encoding:
This transforms categorical features into numerical representations, by creating a binary feature for each unique value in the category. This is essential for algorithms that only accept numerical inputs. For example, the categorical variable "color" with values "red," "green," and "blue" would be transformed into three binary features: "is_red," "is_green," and "is_blue."

Binning:
This groups continuous features into discrete intervals or bins. This can be useful for simplifying the data and dealing with outliers. For example, ages could be grouped into bins like "18-25," "26-35," "36-45," etc.

Polynomial features:
Adding polynomial features (e.g., squaring or cubing existing features) can capture non-linear relationships in the data. However, be mindful of overfitting; too many polynomial features can increase the model's complexity unnecessarily.

Interaction features:
Creating new features by combining existing features can capture interactions between variables. For example, the interaction between "temperature" and "humidity" might be a strong predictor of "crop yield."

Feature selection, on the other hand, is the process of choosing a subset of relevant features from the initial set, aiming to improve model performance and reduce complexity. This is particularly important when dealing with high-dimensional data (many features), as irrelevant or redundant features can hinder model training and increase computational costs. Many techniques exist for feature selection, each with its strengths and weaknesses.

Filter methods:
These methods rank features based on statistical measures of their relationship with the target

variable, independently of the chosen learning algorithm. Examples include correlation coefficients, chi-squared tests, mutual information, and ANOVA. Features with low scores are discarded. These methods are computationally efficient and less prone to overfitting.

Wrapper methods:
These methods evaluate subsets of features by training a model on each subset and selecting the subset that yields the best performance. Examples include recursive feature elimination (RFE) and forward/backward selection. These methods are more computationally
expensive but often lead to better performance compared to filter methods, as they consider the interaction between features.

Embedded methods:
These methods perform feature selection during the model training process. Examples include L1 regularization (LASSO) and decision tree-based methods. LASSO penalizes the use of many features by adding a penalty term to the loss function, effectively
shrinking the coefficients of less important features to zero. Decision trees implicitly perform feature selection by prioritizing features that provide the most information gain at each node.

The choice of feature engineering and selection techniques depends heavily on the specific problem, dataset, and model. Experimentation and iterative refinement are key to finding the optimal combination of techniques. It is not uncommon to spend significantly more time on feature engineering and selection than on selecting and training the model itself. Remember to evaluate the performance of your model thoroughly after each iteration of feature engineering and selection, using appropriate evaluation metrics, to ensure that the changes are improving, rather than harming, the overall performance. The process is iterative: you may find that a new feature reveals the importance of another, unseen relationship that needs further engineering. The ultimate goal is to create a model that is both accurate and interpretable. Overly complex features might make the model powerful but completely opaque in its decision-making, while overly simple features might lead to a model that is interpretable but fails to capture the nuances of the data. The sweet spot is finding that balance.

Finally, remember the importance of data preprocessing. Before starting any feature engineering or selection, it's crucial to clean the data. This involves handling missing values, dealing with outliers, and ensuring data consistency. Techniques like imputation (filling missing values), outlier detection and removal, and data transformation are essential steps to ensure the quality of your dataset before moving on to the more sophisticated techniques of feature engineering and selection. Neglecting this crucial step can lead to biases in the model and adversely affect its performance. The preprocessing stage often involves understanding the nature of missing data—is it missing completely at random (MCAR), missing at random (MAR), or missing not at random (MNAR)—to select the appropriate imputation technique. Each case requires a different approach, and selecting the wrong technique could introduce significant bias into the final model. The choice of imputation technique, therefore, should be made judiciously, considering the data's characteristics and potential consequences of bias introduction.

In conclusion, feature engineering and selection are critical components in building effective machine learning models. They are iterative processes requiring a deep understanding of the problem domain, creative problem-solving, and rigorous evaluation. By mastering these techniques, data scientists can transform raw data into powerful features, leading to models that are not only accurate but also efficient and interpretable. The careful selection of features can significantly improve model performance and reduce computational cost, ultimately leading to more reliable and robust AI systems. The journey from raw data to a deployed model is rarely linear, involving numerous rounds of experimentation, refinement, and validation, with feature engineering and selection playing a pivotal role throughout.

Perceptrons and Multilayer Perceptrons

The journey into the heart of neural networks begins with understanding their fundamental building blocks: perceptrons. A perceptron, at its core, is a simplified model of a biological neuron. It takes multiple inputs, each weighted by a corresponding coefficient, sums these weighted inputs, and then applies an activation function to produce an output. Think of it as a decision-making unit: if the weighted sum exceeds a certain threshold, it fires (outputs 1); otherwise, it remains silent (outputs 0). This seemingly simple structure forms the basis for far more complex neural networks.

Mathematically, a perceptron's operation can be expressed as:

`output = f(Σ(wᵢxᵢ + b))`

Where:

`xᵢ` represents the input values.
`wᵢ` represents the corresponding weights assigned to each input. These weights determine the influence of each input on the final output. Learning in a perceptron essentially involves adjusting these weights.
`b` is the bias term, a constant that adds an offset to the weighted sum. This allows the perceptron to activate even when all inputs are zero.
`f` is the activation function, a non-linear function that introduces complexity and allows the perceptron to model non-linear relationships. Common activation functions include the step function (the simplest, producing a binary output), the sigmoid function (producing a continuous output

between 0 and 1), and the ReLU (Rectified Linear Unit) function (producing 0 for negative inputs and the input value itself for positive inputs).

The choice of activation function significantly impacts the perceptron's behavior and the type of problems it can effectively solve. The step function, while simple, is limited in its ability to model complex patterns. The sigmoid function, on the other hand, provides a smooth, differentiable output, making it suitable for gradient-based learning algorithms. ReLU, with its simplicity and efficiency in training, has become a popular choice in many modern neural networks.

Let's consider a simple example: Imagine a perceptron designed to classify whether a student will pass or fail an exam based on two inputs: hours studied (x_1) and test score on a practice exam (x_2). We could assign weights to these inputs (e.g., $w_1 = 0.5$, $w_2 = 0.8$) representing their relative importance. A higher weight suggests a stronger influence on the final decision. The bias term (b) could be set to -5. If we use a step function as the activation function, the perceptron would output 1 (pass) if $0.5 x_1 + 0.8 x_2 - 5 > 0$ and 0 (fail) otherwise. The weights and bias would be adjusted through training to optimize the perceptron's performance on a dataset of student exam results.

While perceptrons are effective for linearly separable problems (problems where data can be separated by a single line or hyperplane), they struggle with complex, non-linearly separable datasets. This limitation is overcome by using multilayer perceptrons (MLPs), also known as feedforward neural networks.

An MLP extends the functionality of a single perceptron by arranging multiple perceptrons in layers. A typical MLP consists of an input layer, one or more hidden layers, and an output layer. The input layer receives the initial data, each hidden layer processes the data through weighted sums and activation functions, and the output layer produces the final prediction or classification. The connections between layers are weighted, and the learning process involves adjusting these weights to minimize the error between predicted and actual outputs.

The introduction of hidden layers is crucial for the power of MLPs. Each hidden layer learns increasingly complex representations of the input data, allowing the network to model non-linear relationships. For instance, the first hidden layer might learn simple features from the input, while subsequent layers combine these features to learn more abstract representations. This hierarchical representation learning is a key factor contributing to the success of deep learning models.

The training process of an MLP involves forward propagation and backpropagation. Forward propagation involves feeding the input data through the network layer by layer, calculating the output of each neuron based on its weighted inputs and activation function. This process produces the network's prediction. Backpropagation, on the other hand, calculates the error between the predicted output and the actual target value and then propagates this error back through the network, adjusting the weights in each layer to reduce the error. This iterative process of forward propagation, error calculation, and weight adjustment continues until the network's performance reaches a satisfactory level.

The choice of optimization algorithm plays a vital role in the efficiency and effectiveness of the backpropagation process. Gradient descent is a widely used algorithm that iteratively updates the weights by moving them in the direction of the negative gradient of the error function. Variations of gradient descent, such as stochastic gradient descent (SGD) and Adam, offer improvements in terms of convergence speed and efficiency.

Building an MLP involves several design choices. The number of hidden layers and the number of neurons in each layer are important hyperparameters that affect the network's capacity to learn complex patterns. Too few layers or neurons might lead to underfitting (the network failing to capture the underlying patterns in the data), while too many might lead to overfitting (the network memorizing the training data rather than learning generalizable patterns).

The activation function used in the hidden layers also influences the network's behavior. ReLU, due to its efficiency and avoidance of the vanishing gradient problem (where gradients become very small during backpropagation, hindering learning), is often preferred in hidden layers. The output layer's activation function depends on the type of problem being solved. For binary classification problems, the sigmoid function is a common choice, while for multi-class classification problems, the softmax function is frequently used.

Let's illustrate with a practical example. Suppose we want to build an MLP to classify images of handwritten digits (0-9) using the MNIST dataset. This dataset contains thousands of images, each labeled with the corresponding digit. We would first preprocess the images, perhaps converting them to grayscale and normalizing the pixel intensities. Then, we would design an MLP with an input layer representing the flattened image pixels, one or more hidden layers using ReLU activation functions, and an output layer with 10 neurons (one for each digit) using a softmax activation function. The training process would involve feeding the network the preprocessed images and their labels, calculating the error, and adjusting the weights using an optimization algorithm like Adam. We would monitor the network's performance on a separate validation set to avoid overfitting and ensure generalization to unseen data.

The creation of an MLP, from defining the architecture to selecting the appropriate activation functions and optimization algorithms, represents a blend of art and science. Experimentation and careful tuning of hyperparameters are essential for achieving optimal performance. Understanding the fundamental principles of perceptrons and the architecture of MLPs forms a crucial foundation for venturing into the more complex world of deep learning architectures like convolutional neural networks (CNNs) and recurrent neural networks (RNNs), which will be explored in subsequent chapters. The principles underlying the simple perceptron and its extension into the MLP lay the groundwork for understanding the power and flexibility of deep learning models. Mastering these fundamentals is key to unlocking the potential of AI. The seemingly simple perceptron, in its elegant design, provides the building blocks for incredibly sophisticated artificial intelligence systems. Understanding its limitations and how the MLP addresses those limitations is crucial for appreciating the advancements in the field of deep learning. This foundational knowledge will prove invaluable as we delve into more complex neural network architectures in later chapters.

Sigmoid ReLU and Others

The perceptron, as we've seen, is a fundamental building block, but it's the activation function that breathes life into it, introducing non-linearity and enabling the network to learn complex patterns. Without an activation function, a multi-layer perceptron (MLP) would simply be a linear transformation of the input data, severely limiting its capacity to model intricate relationships. The choice of activation function significantly impacts the network's learning ability, convergence speed, and overall performance. Let's delve into some of the most prevalent choices.

The sigmoid function, also known as the logistic function, is a classic and historically important activation function. Mathematically represented as $\sigma(x) = 1 / (1 + \exp(-x))$, it outputs a value between 0 and 1. This characteristic makes it suitable for binary classification problems, where the output represents the probability of belonging to a particular class. Its S-shaped curve provides a smooth transition, making it relatively easy to optimize during training. However, the sigmoid function suffers from a significant drawback: the vanishing gradient problem. As the magnitude of the input increases, either positively or negatively, the gradient of the function approaches zero. This means that during backpropagation, the updates to the network's weights become increasingly smaller, hindering the learning process, particularly in deep networks where the gradient signal needs to propagate through many layers. The vanishing gradient problem effectively slows down or completely stalls the learning process, making the training process inefficient and unreliable for deeper networks. This is one of the reasons why other activation functions have largely superseded the sigmoid in many applications. The sigmoid's tendency to saturate (output values close to 0 or 1) also contributes to the vanishing gradient problem, leading to slow or stalled learning. While historically important, the sigmoid's limitations have spurred the search for more effective alternatives.

The Rectified Linear Unit (ReLU), defined as ReLU(x) = max(0, x), has become incredibly popular due to its simplicity and effectiveness. It outputs the input directly if the input is positive, and zero otherwise. This simple yet powerful function avoids the vanishing gradient problem largely associated with the sigmoid and tanh functions. For positive inputs, the gradient is consistently 1, allowing for efficient backpropagation even in deep networks. The simplicity of ReLU also translates to faster computation compared to sigmoid or tanh, offering a significant advantage in training deep neural networks. However, ReLU is not without its shortcomings. The "dying ReLU" problem occurs when a neuron's weight updates consistently lead to negative inputs. This causes the neuron to consistently output zero, effectively "dying" and failing to contribute to the network's learning process. This phenomenon is particularly prevalent in situations where the learning rate is too high or the weights are initialized poorly. Consequently, some neurons might become inactive throughout the training process, resulting in the network failing to reach its full potential. Various modifications have been proposed to address the dying ReLU problem.

One such modification is Leaky ReLU (LReLU), which aims to alleviate the dying ReLU problem by introducing a small slope for negative inputs. The equation for LReLU is typically represented as LReLU(x) = max(αx, x), where α is a small positive constant (e.g., 0.01). This modification ensures that the gradient is never exactly zero, helping to prevent neurons from becoming completely inactive. The value of α can be either a fixed constant or learned during the training process. The introduction of this small slope provides a non-zero gradient for negative inputs, preventing the neuron from completely shutting down during training, improving the robustness and learning ability of the network. This is especially important in deeper networks, as it helps to prevent the vanishing gradient problem from occurring.

Another variation is Parametric ReLU (PReLU), which takes this concept a step further by allowing the slope for negative inputs (α) to be a learnable parameter. Instead of being a predefined constant, α is learned during the training process, allowing the network to adapt the slope for negative inputs to best suit the data. This dynamic adjustment of the slope provides increased flexibility and allows the network to learn more complex representations. This adaptation offers a level of self-regulation, optimizing the network's response to negative inputs more effectively than the fixed slope used in Leaky ReLU. Experimentally, PReLU often yields better performance than Leaky ReLU, demonstrating the advantages of learning the slope parameter.

Beyond ReLU and its variants, other activation functions have been proposed and applied. The Exponential Linear Unit (ELU) aims to address the dying ReLU problem while also pushing the mean activations closer to zero, which can help with faster training. $ELU(x) = x$ if $x > 0$, and $\alpha(\exp(x) - 1)$ if $x \leq 0$, where α is a hyperparameter. This function combines the advantages of ReLU while mitigating its shortcomings, making it a competitive choice in various applications. The ability of ELU to avoid the dying ReLU problem and its effect on mean activations contribute to improved training efficiency and overall network performance.

The softplus function, a smoothed version of ReLU, is another option. Defined as softplus(x) = ln(1 + exp(x)), it provides a continuous approximation of ReLU. While offering smoother gradients than ReLU, it's computationally more expensive and might not offer significant advantages in many applications. Softplus's smoothness makes it suitable for certain tasks, but this advantage is often outweighed by its increased computational demands. This often results in slower training and a less significant improvement over other functions that strike a better balance between smoothness and efficiency.

The choice of activation function is not a trivial matter. It depends heavily on the specific task, network architecture, and dataset characteristics. Empirical experimentation is crucial in finding the best activation function for a given problem. In some cases, using different activation functions for different layers within the network can improve performance. For instance, combining ReLU in hidden layers with a sigmoid or softmax in the output layer for binary or multi-class classification respectively is a common practice. The selection and tuning of these hyperparameters, like the choice of activation functions, often require a degree of informed experimentation to determine the optimal configuration for a particular task.

Beyond the aforementioned functions, the development of new activation functions is an active area of research. The search for activation functions that are robust, efficient, and better suited for specific problem domains continues to drive innovation in deep learning. The exploration of novel activation functions represents an ongoing pursuit to enhance the capabilities and efficiency of neural networks. The landscape of activation functions is dynamically evolving, reflecting the ongoing quest for more efficient and robust neural network architectures.

In summary, the activation function plays a crucial role in the functionality of neural networks. The selection of an appropriate activation function is vital for the successful training and effective deployment of a neural network. While ReLU and its variants have gained significant popularity due to their efficiency and ability to address the vanishing gradient problem, the choice ultimately depends on the specifics of the task at hand and often requires experimentation to determine the best fit. Understanding the strengths and weaknesses of various activation functions provides a foundation for building more effective and robust AI systems. The careful consideration of activation functions underscores the intricate interplay between theory and practice in the development of successful AI models.

Forward and Backward Propagation

Having established the foundational role of activation functions in imbuing neural networks with the capacity to learn complex patterns, we now turn our attention to the very heart of the neural network training process: forward and backward propagation. These two processes, intertwined in a continuous feedback loop, are the engines that drive the learning process, allowing the network to progressively refine its internal parameters and improve its predictive accuracy.

Forward propagation, as the name suggests, involves the systematic flow of information through the network, from the input layer to the output layer. Imagine a wave propagating through a medium; similarly, the input data, represented as a vector, is fed into the input layer of the network. Each neuron in a layer receives weighted sums of the outputs from the preceding layer. These weighted sums are then passed through the neuron's activation function, producing an output that is then passed on to the next layer. This process continues until the signal reaches the output layer, generating a prediction. Let's visualize this with a simple example:

Consider a simple two-layer neural network tasked with classifying images of handwritten digits (like the MNIST dataset). The input layer receives a flattened vector representing the pixel intensities of an image. Each connection between neurons in consecutive layers has an associated weight, reflecting the strength of that connection. As the input propagates through the network, each neuron in the hidden layer computes a weighted sum of its inputs, adds a bias term (a constant value), and then applies its activation function (e.g., ReLU). The resulting activations are then passed to the output layer, where a similar computation takes place. The output layer usually employs a softmax function to produce a probability distribution over the possible classes (0-9 in the case of digit classification). This final output represents the network's prediction for the input image.

The beauty of this process lies in its systematic nature. The same calculations are repeated for every neuron in each layer, making it amenable to efficient implementation using matrix operations. This allows us to leverage the power of optimized linear algebra libraries, accelerating the computation and making it feasible to train large and complex networks. Furthermore, the forward pass is completely deterministic; given the network weights, biases, and input data, the output is uniquely determined. This predictability forms the bedrock for the backward propagation process.

Backward propagation, often abbreviated as backprop, is the algorithmic heart of neural network training. It's the process by which the network learns from its mistakes. The forward pass produces a prediction, which is then compared to the actual target value (the ground truth). The discrepancy between the prediction and the ground truth is quantified using a loss function, which measures the error. The goal of backpropagation is to determine how much each weight in the network contributed to this error.

This is achieved through the application of the chain rule of calculus. The chain rule allows us to recursively compute the gradient of the loss function with respect to each weight in the network. The gradient represents the rate of change of the loss function with respect to a particular weight; it tells us how much the error would decrease if we were to slightly adjust that weight. This gradient information is then used to update the weights using an optimization algorithm (e.g., gradient descent, Adam).

Let's delve into the mechanics of backpropagation. The process begins at the output layer. The gradient of the loss function with respect to the output layer's weights is computed. Then, using the chain rule, we propagate this gradient back through the network, calculating the gradients with respect to the weights in the hidden layers. The gradients are computed layer by layer, starting from the output layer and working backwards to the input layer. Each layer receives a "delta" term, which represents the contribution of that layer to the overall error. This process ensures that the updates to the weights are proportionate to their contribution to the error.

Several factors significantly influence the efficiency and effectiveness of backpropagation. One critical factor is the choice of the loss function. Different loss functions are suitable for different types of problems (e.g., mean squared error for regression, cross-entropy for classification). The choice of the activation function in each layer also plays a crucial role. The activation function dictates the non-linearity introduced into the network and can significantly impact the ease of backpropagation, especially in deep networks. The vanishing gradient problem, where the gradients become extremely small during backpropagation in deep networks, can hinder the training process. This is where activation functions like ReLU, which helps mitigate this problem, become crucial.

The optimization algorithm employed also plays a vital role. Gradient descent, with its various modifications (e.g., stochastic gradient descent, mini-batch gradient descent), iteratively updates the network weights based on the calculated gradients. The learning rate, a hyperparameter that controls the step size during weight updates, needs careful tuning. A learning rate that is too large can lead to oscillations and failure to converge, while a learning rate that is too small can result in slow convergence. Advanced optimization algorithms, such as Adam and RMSprop, often demonstrate superior convergence properties compared to standard gradient descent.

The process of forward and backward propagation is iterative. The network repeatedly performs forward propagation to generate predictions, followed by backward propagation to compute gradients and update weights. This iterative process continues until the network reaches a satisfactory level of performance, as measured by the loss function on a validation set, or until a predetermined number of iterations have been completed. It's important to emphasize that the convergence of the network is not guaranteed; it depends on several factors, including the network architecture, the choice of hyperparameters, the quality of the training data, and the presence of noise in the data.

The interplay between forward and backward propagation is the engine driving the learning process in neural networks. Forward propagation systematically propagates the input data through the network to generate predictions, while backward propagation uses the prediction error to refine the network's weights, enabling it to learn from data and improve its performance. The effective implementation of these processes requires a deep understanding of calculus, linear algebra, and the careful consideration of various design choices like the choice of activation function, loss function, and optimization algorithm. The interplay between these components highlights the elegant but intricate process of neural network training. The ability to effectively leverage this interplay is a cornerstone of successful AI development.

Mastering these concepts empowers you to build sophisticated and powerful AI systems capable of solving complex real-world problems. Further exploration into regularization techniques and other advanced optimization strategies will further enhance your ability to train robust and efficient neural networks. The synergy between these fundamental processes forms the core of the remarkable power of neural networks in the field of artificial intelligence.

Gradient Descent and Variants

Having understood the mechanics of forward and backward propagation, we now arrive at a crucial component of training neural networks: optimization algorithms. These algorithms dictate how the network adjusts its internal parameters (weights and biases) to minimize the error between its predictions and the actual target values. The goal is to find the optimal set of weights and biases that yield the lowest possible error, thus maximizing the network's accuracy. A fundamental algorithm in this process is gradient descent.

Gradient descent is an iterative optimization algorithm that aims to find the minimum of a function. In the context of neural networks, this function is the loss function, which quantifies the error between the network's predictions and the ground truth. The algorithm works by taking steps in the direction of the negative gradient of the loss function. The gradient, in essence, points towards the direction of the steepest ascent; by moving in the opposite direction (negative gradient), we descend towards the minimum.

Imagine a hiker trying to reach the bottom of a valley in a fog. They can't see the entire valley, only the immediate surroundings. At each point, they look around and take a step downhill in the steepest direction. This process is analogous to gradient descent: the hiker's position represents the current set of weights and biases, the valley represents the loss function landscape, and the steps downhill represent the updates to the weights and biases.

Mathematically, the gradient descent update rule is expressed as:

$$\theta = \theta - \eta \nabla L(\theta)$$

where:

θ represents the vector of weights and biases.
η is the learning rate, a hyperparameter controlling the step size. A smaller learning rate leads to smaller steps, potentially resulting in slower convergence but potentially avoiding overshooting the minimum. A larger learning rate can speed up convergence but risks overshooting and failing to converge.
$\nabla L(\theta)$ is the gradient of the loss function with respect to θ. This gradient is computed using backpropagation.

The choice of learning rate is critical. A learning rate that is too small can lead to excessively slow convergence, while a learning rate that is too large can cause the algorithm to oscillate or diverge, failing to find a minimum. Finding the optimal learning rate often involves experimentation and techniques like learning rate scheduling, where the learning rate is adjusted during training.

While standard gradient descent considers the entire training dataset to compute the gradient at each iteration, this can be computationally expensive for large datasets. This motivates the use of stochastic gradient descent (SGD).

Stochastic gradient descent (SGD) addresses the computational burden of gradient descent by approximating the gradient using only a small subset of the training data, called a mini-batch, at each iteration. Instead of calculating the gradient based on the entire dataset, SGD randomly samples a mini-batch and computes the gradient using only the data points within that mini-batch. This significantly reduces the computational cost per iteration, allowing for faster training. The randomness introduced by sampling mini-batches also helps the algorithm escape local minima, which are points that appear to be minima but are not the global minimum.

However, the stochastic nature of SGD can introduce noise in the gradient estimation, leading to oscillations around the minimum. This can be mitigated by using techniques like momentum and adaptive learning rates.

Momentum aims to smooth out the oscillations in SGD by incorporating information from previous gradient updates. The update rule with momentum incorporates a momentum term, which is a weighted average of past gradients. This allows the algorithm to continue moving in a consistent direction even if the current gradient is noisy.

Adaptive learning rates adjust the learning rate for each weight individually based on the history of gradients for that weight. Popular algorithms that employ adaptive learning rates include AdaGrad, RMSprop, and Adam.

AdaGrad adapts the learning rate for each parameter based on the historical sum of squared gradients. It reduces the learning rate for parameters with large gradients and increases it for parameters with small gradients. This can be beneficial for sparse data, where some parameters may receive infrequent updates. However, AdaGrad can become too conservative as the training progresses and accumulate a sum of squared gradients which may become too large, effectively stopping the optimization process.

RMSprop (Root Mean Square Propagation) addresses the diminishing learning rate problem of AdaGrad by using an exponentially decaying average of past squared gradients instead of the cumulative sum. This allows the learning rate to adapt more effectively throughout the training process. RMSprop's update step is usually faster than AdaGrad.

Adam (Adaptive Moment Estimation) combines the ideas of momentum and adaptive learning rates. It maintains estimates of both the first moment (mean) and the second moment (uncentered variance) of the gradients, using exponentially decaying averages. Adam generally performs well and is often the default choice for many applications. Its adaptive learning rate and momentum characteristics combine to efficiently navigate the loss function landscape.

The choice of optimization algorithm often depends on the specific problem and dataset. While SGD with momentum or Adam often offer a good starting point, experimentation and careful consideration of the algorithm's properties are essential to achieve optimal performance.

Beyond these fundamental algorithms, numerous variations and advanced optimization techniques exist. These include techniques like Nesterov accelerated gradient, which adds a lookahead term to the momentum update, and methods that address specific challenges such as saddle points, where the gradient is zero but the point is not a minimum.

The selection of the appropriate optimization algorithm is a crucial hyperparameter tuning step in the neural network training process. Experimentation with different algorithms and careful monitoring of the training process are key to determining the most effective method for a given task. The performance of your neural network is intimately linked to the choice of optimization algorithm, highlighting its central role in the training process. The ability to select and effectively utilize these optimization techniques significantly impacts the efficiency and accuracy of your AI models.

Building a Simple MLP Classifier

Now that we've explored the theoretical underpinnings of neural networks and the optimization algorithms driving their learning, let's put our knowledge into practice. We'll build a simple Multi-Layer Perceptron (MLP) classifier using a small, easily understandable dataset. This hands-on exercise will solidify our comprehension of the concepts discussed and provide a foundational understanding for tackling more complex models later.

Our chosen dataset will be a synthetically generated one, allowing us to control its characteristics and understand the behavior of the MLP more clearly. Let's generate a dataset with two input features (x1 and x2) and one output label (y). The label will be binary (0 or 1), making this a binary classification problem. We'll use the NumPy library in Python, a cornerstone of numerical computation in the field of data science and AI.

```python
import numpy as np
```

Generate a synthetic dataset

np.random.seed(42) for reproducibility
num_samples = 100
x1 = np.random.rand(num_samples)
x2 = np.random.rand(num_samples)
y = np.where(x1 + x2 > 1, 1, 0) Linearly separable data

Reshape the input features to be suitable for the neural network.

X = np.column_stack((x1, x2))
```

This code snippet generates 100 data points. Each data point has two features, `x1` and `x2`, randomly sampled from a uniform distribution between 0 and 1. The label `y` is determined by a simple linear rule: if the sum of `x1` and `x2` is greater than 1, the label is 1; otherwise, it's 0. This creates a linearly separable dataset, meaning a simple line can perfectly separate the data points belonging to class 0 from those belonging to class 1. This simplification allows us to easily visualize the decision boundary learned by our MLP. The `np.column_stack` function combines `x1` and `x2` into a single matrix `X`, which is the standard input format for our neural network. The `np.random.seed(42)` line ensures that the random numbers generated are consistent each time the code is run, making the results reproducible.

Next, we'll build our MLP using TensorFlow/Keras, a powerful and user-friendly framework for building and training neural networks. We'll opt for a simple architecture with an input layer, a hidden layer, and an output layer.

```python
import tensorflow as tf
from tensorflow import keras

# Define the MLP model

model = keras.Sequential([
keras.layers.Dense(10, activation='sigmoid', input_shape=(2,)), Input layer and hidden layer
keras.layers.Dense(1, activation='sigmoid') Output layer ])

# Compile the model

model.compile(optimizer='sgd',
loss='binary_crossentropy',
metrics=['accuracy'])

# Train the model

```
model.fit(X, y, epochs=100, verbose=1)
```
```

Here, we define a sequential model with two dense layers. The first layer has 10 neurons (units) and uses the sigmoid activation function. The input shape is specified as (2,), indicating two input features. The second layer has a single neuron (as it's a binary classification problem) and also uses a sigmoid activation function. Sigmoid is a popular choice for binary classification because its output is bounded between 0 and 1, representing probabilities. The `compile` method specifies the optimization algorithm ('sgd' – stochastic gradient descent), the loss function ('binary_crossentropy', suitable for binary classification), and the evaluation metric ('accuracy'). Finally, `model.fit` trains the model on our dataset for 100 epochs. `verbose=1` provides a progress bar during training.

Let's expand on the choices made in this code. The selection of the sigmoid activation function deserves further explanation. The sigmoid function, defined as $1 / (1 + \exp(-x))$, outputs a value between 0 and 1, making it ideal for representing probabilities in a binary classification context. Its S-shaped curve introduces non-linearity into the model, allowing it to learn complex relationships between inputs and outputs that wouldn't be possible with a purely linear model. Other activation functions, such as ReLU (Rectified Linear Unit), tanh (hyperbolic tangent), and softmax, are common alternatives depending on the specific task and network architecture. The selection of an appropriate activation function is a crucial part of designing effective neural networks.
```

The choice of the 'sgd' optimizer is also significant. Stochastic gradient descent iteratively updates the weights of the network based on the gradients of the loss function computed on small batches of training data. This approach is computationally efficient, especially for large datasets. Other optimizers like Adam, RMSprop, and Adagrad offer different approaches to gradient descent, potentially leading to faster convergence or better performance in specific situations. The selection of an appropriate optimizer is an essential part of model optimization and should be based on the particular challenges and data set characteristics.

Furthermore, the `binary_crossentropy` loss function measures the dissimilarity between the predicted probabilities and the true labels. It's a widely used loss function for binary classification problems, designed to optimize the model's ability to accurately predict the probability of belonging to one of two classes. Other loss functions, such as mean squared error, hinge loss, and Kullback-Leibler divergence, exist, each appropriate for different machine learning scenarios. Choosing the right loss function is crucial to ensure the model learns the intended task effectively. The selection of loss function, optimizer, and activation function are all hyperparameters that influence the model's performance. Careful experimentation and tuning of these hyperparameters are essential for training effective neural networks.

After training, we can evaluate the model's performance:

```python
loss, accuracy = model.evaluate(X, y, verbose=0) print(f"Loss: {loss:.4f}")
print(f"Accuracy: {accuracy:.4f}")
```

This code evaluates the model on the same dataset it was trained on. While this provides an initial assessment, it's important to note that evaluating only on the training data can lead to overfitting, where the model performs exceptionally well on the training data but poorly on unseen data. To mitigate overfitting, we would typically split our data into training and testing sets, training the model only on the training set and evaluating its performance on the held-out testing set.

This simple example provides a hands-on experience in building and training a basic MLP classifier. While this MLP handles our linearly separable dataset effectively, more complex datasets require more sophisticated architectures and techniques, such as deeper networks, different activation functions, regularization methods (to prevent overfitting), and more advanced optimization algorithms. This foundation, however, serves as an essential stepping stone to understanding and building more powerful neural networks. The ability to interpret and adapt these fundamental elements is critical to success in building effective AI systems. Moving forward, we will explore more advanced architectures and techniques to address the limitations of this simple model and to tackle a broader range of complex machine learning tasks.

Introduction to CNN Architecture

Convolutional Neural Networks (CNNs) represent a significant advancement in the field of deep learning, particularly excelling in image recognition, object detection, and image segmentation tasks. Unlike Multilayer Perceptrons (MLPs) which treat input data as a flat vector, CNNs leverage the inherent spatial structure present in images. This spatial understanding allows CNNs to effectively capture features and patterns within images, leading to superior performance compared to traditional methods. The core strength of CNNs lies in their architecture, which incorporates specialized layers designed to extract meaningful features from visual data. These layers are the convolutional layer and the pooling layer, working synergistically to build a robust representation of the image.

The convolutional layer is the fundamental building block of a CNN. It employs a set of filters, also known as kernels, that are small matrices of weights. These filters are slid across the input image, performing an element-wise multiplication with the corresponding section of the image (called a receptive field). The result of this multiplication is then summed, producing a single value. This process, known as convolution, extracts local features from the image. For example, a filter might be designed to detect edges, corners, or specific textures. The filter's weights are learned during the training process, adapting to optimally capture relevant features from the training data. The number of filters in a convolutional layer determines the richness of the feature representation; more filters allow for the detection of a wider range of features. The dimensionality of the filter (e.g., 3x3, 5x5) determines the size of the receptive field and the level of detail captured. A larger filter captures larger-scale features, while smaller filters capture finer details.

Consider a 3x3 filter applied to a grayscale image. Each element in the filter corresponds to a weight, and the filter moves systematically across the input image. For each position, the element-wise multiplication is computed, the results are summed, and a single output value is generated. This output value represents the activation of the filter at that specific location in the image. By repeatedly applying the filter to every possible location within the image, we generate a feature map. This feature map captures the presence and strength of the specific feature detected by the filter across the entire image. Multiple filters can be applied in parallel within a single convolutional layer. This allows for the simultaneous detection of multiple features, creating multiple feature maps, each reflecting a different aspect of the image. For example, one filter might detect vertical edges, while another detects horizontal edges, resulting in two distinct feature maps.

The output of a convolutional layer typically undergoes further processing via a pooling layer. The purpose of the pooling layer is to reduce the dimensionality of the feature maps produced by the convolutional layers, resulting in a smaller representation of the image while preserving important features. This dimensionality reduction offers several advantages: it reduces the computational cost of subsequent layers, makes the model more robust to small variations in the input image (e.g., slight shifts in object position), and helps prevent overfitting.

Common pooling operations include max pooling and average pooling. Max pooling selects the maximum value from a specified region (pooling window) within a feature map. Average pooling calculates the average value within the pooling window. Both methods effectively reduce the size of the feature map while emphasizing the most prominent features. For example, a 2x2 max pooling operation will reduce a 10x10 feature map into a 5x5 feature map, where each element represents the maximum value within a 2x2 region. The choice between max pooling and average pooling often depends on the specific application and dataset, with max pooling frequently being preferred for its tendency to highlight the most salient features.

The combination of convolutional and pooling layers forms the core of a CNN's ability to learn hierarchical features. Initial layers detect simple features like edges and corners. Subsequent layers combine these simple features to detect more complex features like textures and shapes. This process continues in deeper layers, enabling the network to recognize increasingly abstract and complex patterns in the image. This hierarchical representation is crucial for accurate image classification and object recognition. The final layers of the CNN typically consist of fully connected layers, similar to those in an MLP, which perform the final classification or regression task. These layers take the feature representations learned by the convolutional and pooling layers and map them to the output classes.

The architecture of a CNN is highly flexible and adaptable to different tasks and datasets. The number of convolutional and pooling layers, the size of the filters, the type of pooling operation, and the number of neurons in the fully connected layers can all be adjusted to optimize performance. This flexibility allows CNNs to be successfully applied to a wide range of image-related tasks beyond simple image classification. For example, object detection involves identifying the location and class of objects within an image; CNNs can achieve this by utilizing multiple convolutional layers to produce a feature map, followed by a region proposal network (RPN) to identify potential object locations within the image and classifying those regions. Image segmentation, on the other hand, aims to assign a class label to each pixel in the image; CNN architectures like U-Net, which employ an encoder-decoder structure, have proven particularly effective in this task.

The training of a CNN involves optimizing the weights of the filters and neurons in the fully connected layers to minimize a loss function. This is typically achieved using backpropagation and stochastic gradient descent. Backpropagation calculates the gradient of the loss function with respect to the network's weights, and stochastic gradient descent iteratively updates the weights in the direction that reduces the loss. The process involves feeding the network many training examples, calculating the error for each example, and updating the weights based on the error. The MNIST dataset, a collection of handwritten digits, frequently serves as a starting point for learning and experimenting with CNNs due to its relatively small size and ease of access. Training on such datasets allows for hands-on experience in implementing and understanding the workings of a CNN.

Beyond their widespread use in image recognition, CNNs are proving increasingly valuable in various other domains. In natural language processing (NLP), convolutional layers can be used to process sequences of words or characters as one-dimensional images. This approach has shown effectiveness in tasks such as text classification and sentiment analysis. In time-series analysis, CNNs have also shown promise in extracting temporal features and making accurate predictions. The versatility and effectiveness of CNNs highlight their growing significance in the field of deep learning, showcasing the power of adapting the core architecture to various data modalities. The continuing research and development in CNN architectures further promise exciting future advancements, expanding the range of applications and enhancing the capabilities of these powerful models. Understanding the core principles and architecture of CNNs provides a firm foundation for exploring these advanced applications and contributing to the evolution of deep learning itself. Furthermore, the ability to adapt CNNs to various datasets and tasks underscores their versatility and establishes them as a cornerstone of modern AI.

Building an Image Classifier with CNNs using MNIST

We've established the theoretical underpinnings of Convolutional Neural Networks (CNNs), their architectural components, and their advantages over traditional methods like Multilayer Perceptrons (MLPs) for image-related tasks. Now, it's time to put this knowledge into practice. The best way to solidify your understanding is through hands-on experience. We will be building an image classifier using the MNIST dataset, a classic benchmark in the machine learning community. The MNIST dataset comprises a large collection of handwritten digits, offering a perfect testing ground for building and evaluating our CNN model.

The MNIST dataset is readily available through various libraries, including TensorFlow and Keras. Its simplicity in terms of data format and relatively small size make it an excellent choice for beginners. Each image is a 28x28 grayscale image representing a handwritten digit from 0 to 9. This structure perfectly aligns with the strengths of CNNs, enabling us to leverage the spatial relationships between pixels to classify the digits accurately.

Before we dive into the code, let's outline the key steps involved in building our MNIST image classifier using a CNN. First, we'll load the dataset, ensuring that the data is appropriately pre-processed for optimal performance. Pre-processing steps might involve normalization, reshaping, or other transformations depending on the specific needs of our model. For MNIST, normalization to a range between 0 and 1 is a common practice.

Next, we'll design the architecture of our CNN. This includes defining the number of convolutional layers, the number of filters in each layer, the kernel size, the activation function, and the pooling strategy. The choice of these hyperparameters influences the model's capacity to learn complex features and its overall performance. Experimentation and fine-tuning are crucial here to find the optimal configuration for our task. We'll discuss different architectural choices and their trade-offs. A simple CNN might consist of a few convolutional layers followed by max-pooling layers to reduce dimensionality and improve robustness against slight variations in the handwritten digits. The output of these layers will then be flattened and fed into one or more fully connected (dense) layers, which perform the final classification. The final layer uses a softmax activation function to produce probabilities for each of the ten digits (0-9).

Let's proceed with the implementation using TensorFlow/Keras. The code below provides a skeletal structure, allowing you to fill in the specific hyperparameter choices based on your experimental results.

```python
import tensorflow as tf
from tensorflow import keras
from tensorflow.keras.layers import Conv2D, MaxPooling2D, Flatten, Dense
```

Load the MNIST dataset

(x *train, y* train), (x *test, y* test) = keras.datasets.mnist.load_data()

Preprocess the data

```
x_train = x_train.astype("float32") / 255.0
x_test = x_test.astype("float32") / 255.0
x_train = x_train.reshape(-1, 28, 28, 1)  Add channel dimension
x_test = x_test.reshape(-1, 28, 28, 1)

y_train = keras.utils.to_categorical(y_train, num_classes=10)
y_test = keras.utils.to_categorical(y_test, num_classes=10)
```

Define the CNN model

```
model = keras.Sequential([
Conv2D(32, (3, 3), activation='relu', input_shape=(28, 28, 1)),
MaxPooling2D((2, 2)),
Conv2D(64, (3, 3), activation='relu'),
MaxPooling2D((2, 2)),
Flatten(),
Dense(10, activation='softmax')
])
```

Compile the model

```
model.compile(optimizer='adam',
loss='categorical_crossentropy',
metrics=['accuracy'])
```

Train the model

model.fit(x *train, y* train, epochs=10, batch *size=32, validation* data=(x *test, y* test))

Evaluate the model

```
loss, accuracy = model.evaluate(x_test, y_test)
print(f"Test Loss: {loss}")
print(f"Test Accuracy: {accuracy}")
```

```

This code provides a basic CNN architecture. We start with a convolutional layer with 32 filters of size 3x3, followed by max pooling. This process is repeated with 64 filters in the second convolutional layer. The flattened output is then passed to a dense layer with 10 output neurons (one for each digit), using a softmax activation function to obtain probability distributions. The `adam` optimizer and `categorical_crossentropy` loss function are used for training. The model is trained for 10 epochs with a batch size of 32. The test accuracy provides a measure of the model's performance on unseen data.

Let's dissect the code further. The `keras.datasets.mnist.load_data()` function conveniently loads the MNIST dataset into training and testing sets. The data is then preprocessed by normalizing the pixel values to the range [0, 1], a crucial step for many deep learning models. Reshaping adds a channel dimension to the images, which is required by the Conv2D layer. The `to_categorical` function converts the digit labels into one-hot encoded vectors. This representation is necessary for the categorical cross-entropy loss function.

The `keras.Sequential` model allows us to define the network layer by layer. Each layer is an object that takes an input tensor and transforms it into an output tensor. The `Conv2D` layer performs convolution operations, extracting
```

features from the input image. The `MaxPooling2D` layer reduces the spatial dimensions while retaining important features. The `Flatten` layer converts the multi-dimensional output of the convolutional layers into a one-dimensional vector that can be fed into the dense layer. The final dense layer performs the classification task, assigning probabilities to each digit.

The `model.compile` function specifies the optimizer, loss function, and metrics to be used during training. The `adam` optimizer is a popular choice for its efficiency and adaptability. The `categorical_crossentropy` loss function is suitable for multi-class classification problems. The `accuracy` metric provides a measure of the model's performance during training and evaluation.

The `model.fit` function trains the model on the training data. The `epochs` parameter specifies the number of times the entire training dataset is passed through the model. The `batch size` parameter determines the number of samples processed before the model's internal parameters are updated. The `validation data` parameter allows us to monitor the model's performance on a separate validation set during training.

Finally, the `model.evaluate` function evaluates the trained model on the testing dataset, providing the loss and accuracy on unseen data.

This example provides a foundation for building more complex CNN architectures. You can experiment with different hyperparameters, such as the number of layers, filters, kernel size, activation functions, and optimizers, to improve the model's accuracy. You can also explore data augmentation techniques to increase the robustness and generalization ability of your model. Consider adding dropout layers to prevent overfitting. The exploration of different CNN architectures, along with hyperparameter tuning and data augmentation strategies, is a crucial aspect of building effective and efficient image classification models. Experimentation is key to developing an intuitive understanding of how different components contribute to the overall performance. Don't hesitate to modify the code, adding layers, experimenting with different activation functions, and changing the optimizer. Through this process of experimentation and analysis, you will gain a deeper understanding of CNNs and their application in image classification. Remember to analyze your results, interpreting the training curves and accuracy metrics to make informed adjustments. The iterative nature of model development is vital, continually refining your model based on the results obtained. The process of building a CNN and improving its performance is a learning journey in itself, providing invaluable insights into the intricacies of deep learning and model optimization.

Advanced CNN Architectures

Building upon our foundational understanding of CNNs and their application in image classification using the MNIST dataset, we now delve into the fascinating world of advanced CNN architectures. While the simple CNN we constructed provides a solid base, many sophisticated architectures have been developed to address the limitations of simpler models and achieve superior performance on complex image recognition tasks. These advancements often involve innovative approaches to handling depth, width, and the efficient flow of information within the network.

One of the pioneering architectures, and a significant milestone in the field, is AlexNet. Introduced in 2012 by Alex Krizhevsky, Ilya Sutskever, and Geoffrey Hinton, AlexNet dramatically improved the accuracy of image classification on the ImageNet Large Scale Visual Recognition Challenge (ILSVRC). This success was largely attributed to its depth – featuring eight layers, significantly deeper than previous CNNs – and the utilization of rectified linear units (ReLUs) as activation functions. ReLUs, unlike sigmoid or tanh functions, helped mitigate the vanishing gradient problem, allowing for efficient training of deeper networks. AlexNet also employed dropout regularization to prevent overfitting, a common issue in deep learning models. Furthermore, its use of overlapping max-pooling layers reduced computational complexity without significant loss of accuracy. The architecture itself involved convolutional layers interspersed with max-pooling layers, followed by fully connected layers for classification. This combination of deep architecture, ReLUs, dropout, and max-pooling represented a paradigm shift in the field, paving the way for subsequent architectural advancements. The impact of

AlexNet extended far beyond its immediate performance; it served as a blueprint for future research and development in CNN architectures.

Following AlexNet, the VGGNet family of architectures, developed by researchers at the University of Oxford, further refined the design principles. The VGG networks are characterized by their consistent use of small (3x3) convolutional kernels throughout the network. This design choice allows for increased depth with a relatively smaller number of parameters compared to using larger kernels, leading to greater efficiency. Multiple versions of VGGNet exist (VGG16, VGG19, etc.), each differing in depth and the number of convolutional layers. The deeper VGG networks typically achieved higher accuracy but came at the cost of increased computational complexity. The VGG architecture's simplicity and effectiveness made it a popular choice and a strong benchmark for subsequent architectures. Its layered structure, meticulously designed to extract progressively higher-level features from input images, became a standard approach in many future CNN designs. The impact of VGGNet is visible in its widespread adoption for various computer vision tasks and its influence on the design of subsequent architectures.

However, increasing the depth of CNNs presented challenges. The vanishing gradient problem, though mitigated by ReLUs, could still impact performance, and training extremely deep networks became increasingly difficult. ResNet (Residual Networks), introduced by Microsoft Research in 2015, elegantly addressed this issue through the concept of skip connections. ResNet incorporates "residual blocks," which allow gradients to flow more easily through the network, effectively bypassing certain layers. Each residual block contains skip connections, which add the input of the block to its output. This enables the network to learn residual functions instead of trying to learn complex mappings directly. This approach allowed for the training of significantly deeper networks (e.g., ResNet-50, ResNet-101, ResNet-152) without sacrificing performance. The remarkable success of ResNet in ILSVRC demonstrated the power of residual connections in overcoming the limitations of extremely deep CNNs. This breakthrough marked a significant turning point in the field, proving that much deeper networks could be trained effectively and accurately. The impact of ResNet extended beyond simply increased depth. The innovation of residual learning, the ability to allow gradients to flow more efficiently, directly contributed to advancements in training even larger and deeper networks.

Another notable architecture is Inception, developed by Google researchers. Instead of simply increasing the depth or width of the network, Inception utilizes parallel convolutional layers with different kernel sizes. This allows the network to capture features at different scales simultaneously, providing a more robust and comprehensive representation of the input image. The Inception modules, the building blocks of the architecture, combine the outputs of these parallel convolutions. The Inception architecture is notable for its computational efficiency, effectively achieving high performance with a relatively modest number of parameters. Different versions of Inception networks exist (Inception v1, v2, v3, etc.), each incorporating refinements to improve accuracy and efficiency. Inception's innovation lies not just in its parallel convolutional approach but also in its ability to achieve high accuracy with computational efficiency, a crucial factor in deploying deep learning models on resource-constrained devices. The efficient use of computing resources, coupled with the increased feature extraction capabilities, made Inception a significant contribution to the field.

Beyond these major architectures, numerous variations and hybrid approaches have emerged. Researchers constantly explore ways to combine the strengths of different architectures, incorporate novel modules, and adapt them to specific tasks. For example, some architectures integrate attention mechanisms to focus on the most relevant parts of the input image, improving efficiency and performance. Others leverage techniques like dilated convolutions to expand the receptive field of the network without increasing the number of parameters.

The evolution of CNN architectures continues, with a constant push to improve accuracy, efficiency, and robustness. The architectures discussed – AlexNet, VGGNet, ResNet, and Inception – represent significant milestones in this ongoing journey. Understanding these architectures provides a strong foundation for comprehending the more advanced and nuanced developments in the field. They represent a crucial step in understanding the evolution of CNNs, from simpler models to sophisticated architectures capable of handling incredibly complex image recognition tasks with increasing accuracy and efficiency. The key is not to simply memorize these architectures but to understand the design principles behind them – the reasoning behind the choices of kernel sizes, activation functions, connection patterns, and optimization strategies. This conceptual understanding allows for adaptation and innovation in future projects and research.

Furthermore, the development of these architectures is not simply an exercise in theoretical exploration; each improvement has significant practical implications. The increased accuracy of these models translates directly into better performance in various applications such as self-driving cars (object detection), medical image analysis (disease diagnosis), and facial recognition systems (security and identification). The efficiency improvements are equally crucial, making deployment on less powerful hardware feasible, expanding the reach and impact of these technologies.

The choice of which architecture to use for a particular task depends on several factors, including the size and complexity of the dataset, the computational resources available, and the desired level of accuracy. Experimentation and careful evaluation are essential. Often, fine-tuning a pre-trained model on a specific dataset can yield excellent results, saving significant time and computational resources.

Moving forward, understanding the underlying principles that guided the design of these advanced architectures is vital. Analyzing the strengths and weaknesses of each, appreciating their innovative approaches to managing depth, width, and information flow, empowers us to develop our own customized CNN architectures tailored to specific tasks and constraints. The continuous development and refinement of CNN architectures highlight the dynamism and continuous evolution of the field of deep learning. The journey from simpler models to these sophisticated architectures is a testament to the power of iterative research and the pursuit of improved accuracy and efficiency. By understanding these foundational architectures, we're not just studying past successes; we're gaining the tools and insights needed to participate in the ongoing revolution in computer vision. The future of CNNs is a landscape of continuous innovation, and a thorough understanding of these seminal architectures provides a firm foothold for exploring and contributing to this ever-evolving field.

Transfer Learning with CNNs

The limitations of training deep learning models, especially CNNs, from scratch become glaringly apparent when dealing with limited datasets. Gathering and annotating vast amounts of image data is often expensive, time-consuming, and sometimes even impossible. This is where the power of transfer learning shines. Instead of training a CNN from random weights, we leverage the knowledge encoded within a pre-trained model, fine-tuning it to perform a specific task with our relatively small dataset. Think of it as giving your model a head start—a pre-existing vocabulary of visual features learned from millions of images.

Pre-trained models, typically trained on massive datasets like ImageNet, have learned to recognize a wide variety of objects and patterns. These models, often consisting of several convolutional layers followed by fully connected layers, extract hierarchical features from images. Early layers learn basic features like edges and corners, while deeper layers learn more complex features like shapes and objects. This hierarchical representation of features is a key strength of CNNs and the foundation of transfer learning.

The process of transfer learning with CNNs typically involves several steps. First, we select a pre-trained model architecture. Popular choices include VGGNet, ResNet, Inception, and MobileNet. The choice depends on factors like the size of our dataset, the computational resources available, and the desired level of accuracy. VGGNet, for instance, is known for its relatively simple architecture and strong performance, while ResNet architectures are celebrated for their ability to handle very deep networks by employing skip connections to mitigate the vanishing gradient problem. Inception models excel at handling a wide variety of image resolutions efficiently, while MobileNet architectures are optimized for mobile and embedded devices, prioritizing efficiency over raw computational power.

Once a pre-trained model is selected, we load its pre-trained weights. These weights represent the knowledge gained during the initial training on the massive dataset. It's crucial to understand that we're not starting from random weights; we're starting with a model that has already learned a significant amount about image features. This drastically reduces the training time and data requirements for our specific task.

Next, we adapt the pre-trained model to our specific task. This usually involves modifying the final layers of the network. The final layers of a pre-trained model are often specific to the original task, such as classifying 1000 different ImageNet classes. Since our task likely differs, we need to replace these layers with new ones suited to our specific image classification problem. This might involve reducing the number of output neurons to match the number of classes in our dataset. For instance, if our task is to classify cats and dogs, we would replace the final fully connected layer with a layer containing only two output neurons.

The process of replacing or modifying the final layers is often referred to as "fine-tuning." We can freeze the weights of the earlier layers, preventing them from being updated during training. This is because these layers have already learned valuable features that are generally applicable across various image classification tasks. Only the newly added or modified layers will be trained using our limited dataset. This approach is particularly useful when dealing with extremely limited data, as it prevents overfitting to our small dataset.

However, freezing all pre-trained layers might not always yield the best results. In some cases, allowing some of the deeper layers to be fine-tuned can improve performance. This involves unfreezing some of the pre-trained layers and allowing their weights to be updated during training. This allows the model to further refine its feature extraction capabilities specific to our dataset. The number of layers to unfreeze is a hyperparameter that needs to be tuned experimentally. Generally, unfreezing only a few deeper layers is sufficient, particularly with limited data.

The choice of optimizer and learning rate is also crucial in fine-tuning. Lower learning rates are generally preferred, as they allow for more subtle adjustments to the pre-trained weights. A learning rate that is too high might disrupt the knowledge learned during pre-training, leading to poor performance. The Adam optimizer is a popular choice, known for its adaptability and effectiveness in various deep learning tasks.

After fine-tuning, we evaluate the model's performance on a separate validation set, which is a subset of our data held back specifically for evaluation purposes. This helps assess the model's ability to generalize to unseen data. Metrics such as accuracy, precision, recall, and F1-score are used to gauge the model's effectiveness. The performance on the validation set guides adjustments to hyperparameters such as the learning rate, the number of layers to fine-tune, and the choice of optimizer.

Transfer learning significantly accelerates the development of image classifiers, reducing the need for large datasets. This is particularly crucial in domains where obtaining labeled data is challenging or expensive. For example, consider medical image classification. Acquiring a large dataset of accurately annotated medical images can be incredibly difficult and costly due to the need for expert annotation. Transfer learning allows researchers to leverage pre-trained models to build accurate classifiers with a far smaller dataset of medical images.

Let's consider a concrete example. Imagine we're building an image classifier to identify different types of flowers. Gathering a comprehensive dataset of thousands of images representing various flower species is time-consuming and requires expert botanical knowledge for accurate labeling.

Using transfer learning, we can start with a pre-trained model like ResNet50, trained on ImageNet. We replace the final fully connected layer with a layer containing the number of neurons corresponding to the number of flower species we want to classify. We then fine-tune the model using our relatively small flower dataset. The pre-trained model provides a solid foundation, allowing us to achieve reasonable accuracy even with limited data. We might choose to freeze most of the pre-trained layers to prevent overfitting. After training, we evaluate its performance on a held-out validation set and iterate on the hyperparameters until we achieve satisfactory performance.

Another scenario might involve building a system to detect defects in manufactured parts. Collecting and labeling a large dataset of images showing defects in manufacturing processes might be quite challenging. Here again, transfer learning is extremely valuable. A pre-trained model can be leveraged to detect subtle variations and anomalies, even with limited examples of defective parts. We can adapt a pre-trained model by fine-tuning it with images of both defective and non-defective parts. This requires careful selection of the layers to unfreeze to prevent the model from simply learning to classify based on easily discernible characteristics rather than subtle defects.

The versatility and efficiency of transfer learning make it a powerful technique in the deep learning arsenal, especially when dealing with limited resources. By intelligently utilizing pre-trained models, we can significantly reduce the cost, time, and effort required to build high-performing image classifiers, opening up new possibilities in various applications. Moreover, exploring different pre-trained models and fine-tuning strategies adds a layer of customization and optimization crucial for achieving top performance in specific applications. The choice of pre-trained model becomes an integral part of the model design process. The effective use of transfer learning involves understanding the strengths and weaknesses of various pre-trained models and choosing the most appropriate one based on the specific task and available resources. Further exploration into techniques like data augmentation and regularization can further enhance the performance of models built using transfer learning. These techniques help to mitigate overfitting, a common concern when dealing with limited datasets. Therefore, a well-rounded approach to transfer learning involves the judicious selection of pre-trained models, careful fine-tuning strategies, and appropriate data augmentation techniques. Through this combination, we can unlock the full potential of transfer learning and build powerful image classifiers even with limited data.

CNN Applications Beyond Image Classification

Building upon our understanding of convolutional neural networks (CNNs) and their effectiveness in image classification, particularly through the lens of transfer learning, we now venture into their broader applications beyond simple image categorization. While classifying images into predefined categories is a powerful capability, CNNs possess a far richer potential, extending their reach to more complex and nuanced image analysis tasks. Two particularly impactful areas are object detection and image segmentation.

Object detection, unlike image classification, aims to not only identify the presence of objects within an image but also to precisely locate their positions. This involves drawing bounding boxes around detected objects, effectively specifying their spatial extent within the image. This is a significantly more challenging task than mere classification, as the model must simultaneously address both the "what" and the "where" aspects of the image content. Early approaches to object detection often relied on sliding windows, systematically scanning the image with windows of various sizes and applying a classifier to each window. This method, though conceptually straightforward, proved computationally expensive and often yielded suboptimal results.

The advent of deep learning revolutionized object detection. CNN-based architectures, such as Region-based Convolutional Neural Networks (R-CNNs), Fast R-CNNs, Faster R-CNNs, and You Only Look Once (YOLO) networks, offered significant improvements in speed and accuracy. These architectures typically employ a two-stage process: first, a region proposal network (RPN) identifies potential regions of interest (ROIs) within the image that might contain objects. Then, a CNN is applied to each ROI to classify the object and refine the bounding box. Faster R-CNNs improved upon this by integrating the RPN directly into the CNN architecture, enhancing efficiency. YOLO, on the other hand, adopts a single-stage approach, predicting bounding boxes and class probabilities directly from a single CNN pass, thereby achieving significantly higher speeds.

The architectural choices within object detection models are critical. The backbone CNN, often a pre-trained model like ResNet or VGG, extracts features from the image. The head network, built upon the backbone, then processes these features to generate bounding box predictions and class probabilities. Anchors, pre-defined boxes of different sizes and aspect ratios, are frequently used to facilitate the detection of objects at various scales. Non-maximum suppression (NMS) is a crucial post-processing step that eliminates redundant bounding boxes generated by the network, ensuring that only the most confident and non-overlapping predictions are retained. The loss function typically incorporates both classification loss and regression loss for bounding box coordinates. The specific configuration of these components, along with the choice of hyperparameters, significantly influences the performance of the object detection model.

Beyond object detection, image segmentation represents another significant application of CNNs. While object detection identifies and locates objects, image segmentation goes a step further by assigning a label to each pixel in the image, effectively creating a pixel-wise classification map. This allows for a much finer-grained understanding of the image content, accurately delineating the boundaries of objects and differentiating between different regions within the image. There are two primary types of image segmentation: semantic segmentation and instance segmentation.

Semantic segmentation aims to assign a class label to each pixel, identifying the semantic meaning of each pixel. For instance, in a street scene image, semantic segmentation would assign labels like "road," "car," "pedestrian," and "building" to different pixel regions. Instance segmentation, on the other hand, not only classifies each pixel but also distinguishes between individual instances of the same class. In the same street scene example, instance segmentation would separately label each individual car, differentiating them from one another, even if they are of the same class (e.g., "car").

Several architectures are tailored for image segmentation tasks. Fully Convolutional Networks (FCNs) represent a seminal approach, utilizing convolutional layers exclusively to produce a dense pixel-wise prediction map. However, the coarse nature of the predictions initially produced by FCNs led to the development of techniques like upsampling and skip connections to refine the segmentation results. U-Net, a particularly popular architecture for biomedical image segmentation, incorporates a symmetrical encoder-decoder structure with skip connections to effectively capture both context and fine-grained details. Mask R-CNN, a powerful extension of Faster R-CNN, adds a branch to predict pixel-wise masks for each detected object, providing both object detection and instance segmentation capabilities in a unified framework.

The training of image segmentation models usually involves loss functions such as cross-entropy loss, which measures the dissimilarity between the predicted segmentation map and the ground truth mask. Data augmentation techniques, similar to those employed in image classification, play a crucial role in improving the robustness and generalizability of the model. The choice of appropriate evaluation metrics, such as Intersection over Union (IoU) or Dice coefficient, is also vital for assessing the performance of the segmentation model.

The applications of object detection and image segmentation are vast and continually expanding. In autonomous driving, these techniques are crucial for accurately perceiving the surrounding environment, identifying obstacles, and enabling safe navigation. In medical imaging, they aid in the diagnosis of diseases by precisely segmenting organs, tumors, or other relevant structures. In robotics, they enable robots to interact with their environment by recognizing and manipulating objects. In satellite imagery analysis, they assist in tasks such as land cover mapping and urban planning. Even in seemingly unrelated fields like art restoration and historical document analysis, the power of CNNs in object detection and image segmentation is increasingly being harnessed.

Beyond these core applications, CNNs are also finding their way into more specialized and innovative domains. For example, in video analysis, CNNs can be used for action recognition, tracking objects across multiple frames, and generating video summaries. The temporal dimension adds complexity, requiring architectures that can effectively process sequential data, often involving the combination of CNNs with Recurrent Neural Networks (RNNs) or more advanced architectures like 3D CNNs.

The increasing availability of powerful GPUs and specialized hardware accelerators has played a crucial role in making CNN-based object detection and image segmentation feasible and efficient. The computational cost of training and deploying these models can still be substantial, but the advancements in hardware continue to reduce these barriers, widening the accessibility and applicability of CNNs across various sectors. The ongoing research and development in this field promise even more sophisticated and efficient algorithms in the years to come. New architectures, optimized training strategies, and efficient inference methods continuously push the boundaries of what's possible, making CNNs an indispensable tool in the ever-evolving landscape of computer vision and artificial intelligence. The seamless integration of these techniques with other AI components, like natural language processing (NLP), opens up even more exciting avenues for sophisticated AI systems. For instance, imagine an AI system that not only detects and classifies objects in an image but also describes them in natural language, providing a rich and comprehensive understanding of the scene. This highlights the power of combining different AI methodologies to achieve more complex and human-like intelligence. The future of CNNs is bright, with continuous advancements promising even more impactful applications across numerous fields.

Understanding Sequential Data

Sequential data presents a unique set of challenges and opportunities in the realm of machine learning. Unlike the independent and identically distributed (i.i.d.) data commonly assumed in many machine learning algorithms, sequential data points exhibit dependencies across time or order. This temporal dependence is the defining characteristic that distinguishes sequential data from other data types. Understanding this fundamental property is crucial for effectively leveraging the power of Recurrent Neural Networks (RNNs) and their variants, like Long Short-Term Memory (LSTM) networks.

Let's delve into the characteristics of sequential data. The core concept revolves around the temporal or spatial ordering of data points. Each data point, often called a time step or a sequence element, is intrinsically linked to its preceding and succeeding points. This linkage creates a context that is vital for accurate interpretation and prediction. For instance, consider a sentence: "The quick brown fox jumps over the lazy dog." Each word's meaning and the overall sentence's meaning heavily depend on the order of the words. Changing the word order significantly alters the meaning. This inherent ordering is the hallmark of sequential data.

Several types of data fall under the umbrella of sequential data. The most prominent examples include:

Time series data:
This encompasses data collected over time, exhibiting temporal dependencies. Examples include stock prices, weather patterns, sensor readings from IoT devices, and physiological signals like heart rate or

brainwave activity. The value at a given time is inherently connected to the values at previous times. Predicting future values relies heavily on understanding these temporal relationships.

Text data:
Natural language, as exemplified by the sentence above, is quintessential sequential data. The meaning of a sentence or document stems from the sequential arrangement of words, phrases, and sentences. Each word influences the context for subsequent words, forming a complex web of dependencies. This sequential nature is exploited in
numerous NLP tasks like machine translation, sentiment analysis, and text generation.

Speech data:
Similar to text, speech data consists of a
sequence of audio frames, each influencing the interpretation of subsequent frames. Speech recognition systems rely on understanding this temporal ordering to accurately convert audio into text.

Video data:
Video data can be considered a sequence of images,
each frame temporally related to its neighbors.
Action recognition, video classification, and video prediction tasks hinge on understanding the temporal progression of actions and events within the video sequence.

DNA sequences:
In bioinformatics, DNA sequences are represented as strings of nucleotides (A, T, G, C). The order of these nucleotides determines the genetic code and its function. Predicting protein structures and identifying
genetic mutations often involve analyzing the sequential nature of DNA.

The challenges associated with processing sequential data stem directly from its inherent dependencies. Traditional machine learning algorithms, designed primarily for i.i.d.

data, struggle to capture these relationships effectively. For instance, a simple model that treats each word in a sentence independently will fail to understand the overall meaning of the sentence. This is because it ignores the crucial contextual information provided by the sequential arrangement of words.

Another significant challenge is the variable length of sequences. Sentences, speech utterances, and time series data can vary considerably in length. Standard algorithms often require fixed-length inputs, necessitating techniques like padding or truncation, which can introduce noise or lose crucial information. RNNs and LSTMs, however, are explicitly designed to handle variable-length sequences effectively.

Furthermore, the long-range dependencies in sequential data pose a major hurdle. In long sentences or time series, the relationship between distant data points can be crucial for accurate understanding and prediction. However, capturing these long-range dependencies can be difficult due to the vanishing gradient problem, which affects the training of standard RNNs. LSTMs are specifically designed to mitigate this problem, allowing them to learn and maintain long-term dependencies more effectively.

The vanishing gradient problem in standard RNNs arises from the repeated application of the activation function during backpropagation. In simple terms, the gradient signal, which conveys information about the error during training, diminishes exponentially as it propagates through the layers of the network. This means that the model struggles to learn long-range dependencies, as the influence of distant time steps on the current output fades away. LSTMs address this issue through a sophisticated gating mechanism, which regulates the flow of information through the network and prevents the gradient from vanishing.

Let's illustrate these concepts with a practical example. Consider a time series forecasting problem, such as predicting daily stock prices. A naive approach might simply use a linear regression model on past prices. However, this model ignores the inherent temporal dependencies in the data. It might perform poorly because the price on a given day is not only influenced by the previous day's price but also by longer-term trends and external factors. An RNN, on the other hand, can capture these complex dependencies by processing the sequence of past prices and using that information to predict future prices. The model learns the patterns and relationships within the sequential data, resulting in significantly improved forecasting accuracy.

Another example concerns sentiment analysis of movie reviews. The overall sentiment of a review isn't just determined by individual words, but by their interactions and context. A sentence like "This movie was terrible, but the acting was amazing" exhibits conflicting sentiments. A standard bag-of-words model, ignoring the word order, might misclassify the overall sentiment. However, an RNN or LSTM can track the sentiment throughout the review, incorporating the contextual information from preceding words to accurately assess the overall sentiment.

In summary, sequential data presents unique challenges due to its temporal dependencies and variable lengths. Standard machine learning methods often fail to capture these complexities effectively. However, recurrent neural networks, particularly LSTMs, are specifically designed to address these challenges. Their ability to handle variable-length sequences and mitigate the vanishing gradient problem makes them a powerful tool for processing sequential data, enabling applications in diverse fields such as natural language processing, time series analysis, speech recognition, and bioinformatics. The next section will delve into the architecture of basic RNNs and their limitations, setting the stage for a deeper understanding of LSTMs and their superior ability to handle long-range dependencies.

Basic RNN Architecture and Limitations

Recurrent Neural Networks (RNNs) represent a significant advancement in neural network architectures, specifically designed to handle sequential data. Unlike feedforward networks, which process inputs independently, RNNs possess a "memory" mechanism that allows them to consider the context of previous inputs when processing the current one. This inherent ability to maintain a temporal context is what makes them particularly well-suited for tasks involving sequential information, such as natural language processing, speech recognition, and time series forecasting.

At the heart of an RNN lies its recurrent structure, a loop connecting the hidden state at a given time step to the hidden state at the next time step. This loop embodies the network's memory. Let's delve into the mathematical representation to understand this mechanism. The basic RNN architecture can be described by the following equations:

$$h_t = f(W x_t + U h_{t-1} + b)$$

$$y_t = g(V h_t + c)$$

Where:

x_t *represents the input vector at time step t.* This could be a word embedding in NLP, a frame of a video in video analysis, or a data point in a time series.

h_t *represents the hidden state vector at time step t.* This vector acts as the network's memory, encapsulating information from previous time steps. It's the crucial element that differentiates RNNs from feedforward networks.

h_{t-1} represents the hidden state vector from the previous time step ($t-1$). This connection forms the recurrent loop, allowing information to flow across time.

W, **U**, and **V** are weight matrices. W connects the input to the hidden state, U connects the previous hidden state to the current hidden state, and V connects the hidden state to the output.

b and **c** are bias vectors.

$f(.)$ and **$g(.)$** are activation functions, often non-linear functions like tanh or sigmoid. The choice of activation function significantly influences the network's behavior and learning capacity. The hidden state activation function, $f(.)$, is crucial for maintaining the gradient flow during training.

The first equation shows how the hidden state at time t is computed. It's a combination of the current input (

Wx_t), the previous hidden state (Uh_{t-1}), and a bias (b). The activation function, $f(.)$, introduces non-linearity, enabling the network to learn complex relationships between inputs and outputs. The second equation shows how the output at time t (y_t) is generated from the current hidden state (h_t) through a linear transformation (Vh_t) and a bias (c) followed by an activation function, $g(.)$. The output can be a single value, a vector, or a probability distribution depending on the specific application.

Let's consider a simple example: predicting the next word in a sentence. The input x_t would be the word embedding of the current word, h_{t-1} would represent the contextual information derived from the previous words, and y_t would be the probability distribution over all possible next words in the vocabulary. The network iteratively processes the words in the sentence, updating its hidden state at each step and finally predicting the next word based on the accumulated context.

Despite their elegance and ability to model sequential data, basic RNNs suffer from a significant limitation: the vanishing gradient problem. During backpropagation through time (BPTT), the algorithm updates the weights by calculating gradients. However, when dealing with long sequences, the gradients of earlier time steps can become extremely small, effectively hindering the network's ability to learn long-range dependencies. This is because the gradients are repeatedly multiplied by the weight matrices U at each time step. If the eigenvalues of U are less than 1, the repeated multiplication leads to exponentially decreasing gradients, making it difficult to update the weights associated with earlier time steps. This effectively limits the network's ability to "remember" information from the distant past.

Consider a scenario where we are trying to predict the last word of a long sentence. The information relevant to the final prediction might have been presented several words earlier. The vanishing gradient problem means that the network struggles to associate this earlier information with the current prediction because the gradients flowing back from the later time steps to the earlier ones are attenuated exponentially. The network essentially "forgets" what it learned earlier in the sequence.

This vanishing gradient problem severely restricts the effectiveness of basic RNNs in tasks requiring the modeling of long-range dependencies. While the problem is less severe (and can even be reversed, leading to exploding gradients) when the eigenvalues are greater than 1, it still presents a formidable challenge for learning long sequences effectively. The impact of the exploding gradients can be mitigated through techniques such as gradient clipping, which limits the magnitude of the gradients during training. However, this approach only addresses a symptom of the underlying issue, not the root cause. The inherent limitations of the basic RNN architecture in handling long-range dependencies become particularly apparent in applications such as machine translation, where understanding context across entire sentences is crucial.

The vanishing gradient problem arises from the nature of the recurrent connections and the repeated application of the activation function during backpropagation. The repeated multiplication of gradients associated with these recurrent connections can lead to a significant reduction or amplification of the gradients, ultimately impacting the ability to learn effectively.

Another limitation of basic RNNs lies in their computational complexity. The sequential nature of processing necessitates processing each time step one after another, which can be computationally expensive for long sequences. Moreover, the computation required for each time step depends on the length of the sequence, making the complexity of processing increase linearly with sequence length. This contrasts with feedforward networks where the complexity remains roughly constant regardless of input length. This increased computation time is significant for large datasets or complex tasks. Efficient parallelization techniques can alleviate some of these computational burdens but don't completely address the inherent sequential nature of processing in basic RNNs.

These inherent limitations of basic RNN architectures, particularly the vanishing gradient problem and computational cost, motivated the development of more sophisticated recurrent architectures such as Long Short-Term Memory (LSTM) networks and Gated Recurrent Units (GRUs). These advanced architectures incorporate mechanisms to overcome the vanishing gradient problem and enhance their ability to learn long-range dependencies, effectively addressing the limitations of their simpler predecessors. The following sections will explore the architecture and operation of LSTMs and GRUs in detail, demonstrating how they overcome these limitations and provide significant improvements in handling sequential data. We'll also look at practical implementation details and applications of these models, showcasing their effectiveness in real-world scenarios. This deeper dive into LSTMs and GRUs will equip us with the knowledge and skills to design and build powerful AI models capable of handling complex sequential data with high accuracy and efficiency.

Long ShortTerm Memory LSTM Networks

The limitations of standard RNNs, primarily the vanishing gradient problem, severely restrict their capacity to learn long-range dependencies within sequences. This problem arises from the repeated application of the weight matrix during backpropagation through time (BPTT). As gradients are propagated backward through many time steps, they can shrink exponentially, leading to ineffective weight updates for earlier time steps. This means the network struggles to remember information from the distant past, significantly impacting its performance on tasks requiring long-term dependencies, such as translating long sentences or predicting long-term trends in time series data.

Long Short-Term Memory (LSTM) networks were developed to specifically address this vanishing gradient problem. Instead of a single recurrent unit, LSTMs employ a more sophisticated architecture incorporating a cell state, a crucial element that acts as a conveyor belt for information through the network. This cell state runs unchanged through the entire chain, with carefully regulated gates controlling the flow of information into and out of the cell. This clever mechanism enables LSTMs to maintain and process information over extended periods, effectively learning long-range dependencies that would be impossible for standard RNNs.

The core of an LSTM unit comprises three main gates: the input gate, the forget gate, and the output gate. Each gate is a sigmoid function, outputting a value between 0 and 1, representing the degree to which information is allowed to pass through.

The **forget gate** decides what information to discard from the cell state. It receives the previous hidden state (h_{t-1}) and the current input (x_t), and produces a vector f_t (where t represents the current time step). Each element of f_t represents a weight between 0 and 1 assigned to the corresponding element in the previous cell state (C_{t-1}). A value of 0 means completely discarding the information, while a value of 1 means retaining it completely. This weighted sum determines what parts of the previous cell state are forgotten.

The **input gate** determines what new information should be stored in the cell state. This gate has two components: first, a sigmoid layer (i_t) decides which values will be updated, and second, a tanh layer ($\tilde{C}_t$) to add to the cell state.

The updated cell state (C_t) is then calculated by combining the information from the forget gate and the input gate: $C_t = f_t C$

$C_t = f_t * C_{t-1} + i_t * \tilde{C}_t$. This crucial step elegantly balances forgetting irrelevant information and adding new relevant information to the cell state. The carefully controlled flow of information through this process forms the heart of the LSTM's ability to handle long sequences effectively.

Finally, the **output gate** decides what information from the cell state should be output as the hidden state (h_t). A sigmoid layer (o_t) determines which parts of the cell state will be output. This output is then obtained by element-wise multiplying o_t with the tanh of the cell state ($\tanh(C_t)$). This ensures that only relevant portions of the cell state are included in the hidden state, which is then passed on to the subsequent time steps and other layers of the network.

Mathematically, the LSTM can be represented as follows:

Forget Gate:

$$f_t = \sigma(W_f [h_{t-1}, x_t] + b_f)$$

Input Gate:

$$i_t = \sigma(W_i [h_{t-1}, x_t] + b_i)$$

$$\tilde{C}_t = \tanh(W_c [h_{t-1}, x_t$$

$]+b_c)$

Cell State Update:
$$C_t = f_t C_{t-1} + i_t \tilde{C}_t$$

Output Gate:
$$o_t = \sigma(W_o [h_{t-1}, x_t] + b_o)$$

Hidden State:
$$h_t = o_t \tanh(C_t)$$

Where:

σ denotes the sigmoid activation function.
tanh denotes the hyperbolic tangent activation function.
W

W_f, W_i, W_c, W_o are weight matrices.

b_f, b_i, b_c, b_o are bias vectors.

h_{t-1} is the hidden state from the previous time step. x_t is the input at the current time step.

C_{t-1} is the cell state from the previous time step.

C_t is the updated cell state.

h_t is the hidden state at the current time step.

The carefully orchestrated interaction between these gates allows LSTMs to selectively remember or forget information, effectively mitigating the vanishing gradient problem. This selective memory mechanism is crucial for capturing long-range dependencies in sequential data. For instance, in natural language processing, LSTMs can remember information from the beginning of a long sentence when predicting the meaning of words later in the sentence. This ability is significantly superior to standard RNNs, which often lose track of such information due to the vanishing gradient problem.

Let's illustrate with a simple example. Imagine an LSTM processing a sequence of words in a sentence. The forget gate might decide to forget the details of a subject mentioned several sentences earlier if it's no longer relevant to the current context. Conversely, the input gate might add information about a newly introduced character to the cell state. The output gate then carefully selects information from the updated cell state, focusing on what's most pertinent for generating the next word in the sentence. This selective memory allows the LSTM to maintain a coherent understanding of the narrative across the entire sentence, something which standard RNNs struggle to accomplish.

The architecture of LSTMs, with its sophisticated gate mechanisms, allows for efficient gradient flow during backpropagation. The gradients are not repeatedly multiplied across time steps, as they are in basic RNNs. The gates modulate the flow of information through the cell state, preventing the gradients from vanishing or exploding. This contributes significantly to LSTMs' ability to learn long-term dependencies, making them exceptionally well-suited for many sequence modeling tasks.

While LSTMs provide a significant improvement over standard RNNs, they also present computational challenges. The complexity of their architecture leads to higher computational costs compared to basic RNNs. Training LSTMs can therefore be resource-intensive, particularly for very long sequences or large datasets. However, advances in hardware and optimization techniques have mitigated these computational limitations to a large extent, allowing LSTMs to be successfully applied to many complex real-world applications. The benefits in terms of performance and accuracy often outweigh the increased computational cost.

In summary, LSTMs offer a significant step forward in recurrent neural network architectures. Their sophisticated design, characterized by the cell state and carefully regulated gates, effectively addresses the vanishing gradient problem and enables the learning of long-range dependencies in sequential data. This superior ability to capture temporal context makes LSTMs an indispensable tool in a vast range of applications, from machine translation and speech recognition to time-series analysis and music generation. Their effectiveness in handling long sequences and complex patterns has solidified their place as a cornerstone of modern sequence modeling techniques. Understanding the intricacies of LSTMs, and their mechanism for handling sequential data, empowers developers to build robust and accurate AI models for a wide array of applications. The ability to manage and interpret sequential information is key to many of AI's most significant achievements and LSTMs provide a powerful architecture for doing so. The continuing development and refinement of LSTM architectures and training methodologies promise even greater capabilities in the future. Moreover, variants and refinements of LSTMs are actively being researched and developed, promising further improvements in efficiency and performance.

Building an RNN for Text Classification

Now that we've explored the architecture and capabilities of Recurrent Neural Networks (RNNs) and their more advanced cousin, Long Short-Term Memory networks (LSTMs), it's time to put this knowledge into practice. We'll build an RNN for a text classification task, a common and valuable application of RNNs. Text classification involves assigning predefined categories or labels to text documents. This has numerous applications, including spam detection, sentiment analysis, topic categorization, and much more.

Our project will focus on sentiment analysis, determining whether a piece of text expresses positive, negative, or neutral sentiment. We'll use a readily available dataset for this purpose, ensuring reproducibility and allowing us to focus on the implementation details. The choice of dataset will depend on availability and suitability – a balanced dataset with a reasonable size is crucial for effective model training. The IMDB movie review dataset is a popular choice and offers a good starting point.

Before we begin coding, let's reiterate the key components we need to build our RNN. First, we require a suitable dataset. This dataset should consist of text reviews paired with corresponding sentiment labels (positive, negative, neutral). Preprocessing this data is critical; this typically involves tokenization (breaking the text into individual words or sub-words), removing punctuation, handling stop words (common words like "the," "a," "is," which often carry little semantic weight), and converting words into numerical representations using techniques such as one-hot encoding or word embeddings (like Word2Vec or GloVe). Word embeddings are particularly powerful as they capture semantic relationships between words, leading to improved model performance.

Next, we need to design our RNN architecture. We'll use an embedding layer as the input layer to convert the numerical representations of words into a dense vector representation. This layer is followed by the recurrent layer, the heart of our RNN, responsible for processing the sequential nature of text. The recurrent layer's output will feed into a dense layer, followed by a softmax activation function to produce probabilities for each sentiment category (positive, negative, neutral). The softmax function ensures that the output probabilities sum up to 1, representing a probability distribution over the sentiment classes.

The choice of hyperparameters is also important. This includes the number of units in the recurrent layer, the embedding dimension, the learning rate of the optimizer (like Adam or RMSprop), and the number of training epochs. Experimentation and careful tuning of these hyperparameters are vital for optimal performance.

Now let's delve into the Python code using TensorFlow/Keras. First, we'll import the necessary libraries:

```python
import tensorflow as tf
from tensorflow.keras.models import Sequential
from tensorflow.keras.layers import Embedding, LSTM, Dense
from tensorflow.keras.preprocessing.text import Tokenizer
from tensorflow.keras.preprocessing.sequence import pad_sequences
import numpy as np
```

Next, we load and preprocess our dataset. We'll assume we have already downloaded and loaded the IMDB movie review dataset, separating it into training and testing sets. The dataset will be a list of reviews and a corresponding list of labels (0 for negative, 1 for positive; for simplicity, we might ignore neutral sentiment in this example).

```python
```

Assume 'train data' and 'train labels' are loaded from the IMDB dataset

```python
vocab_size = 10000  # Adjust this based on vocabulary size in your dataset
max_length = 100  # Adjust this based on the average review length

tokenizer = Tokenizer(num_words=vocab_size)
tokenizer.fit_on_texts(train_data)
sequences = tokenizer.texts_to_sequences(train_data)
padded_sequences = pad_sequences(sequences, maxlen=max_length)
```

This code snippet tokenizes the reviews, converts words into numerical sequences, and pads the sequences to a uniform length. Padding is essential because RNNs require inputs of a fixed length. We use `num_words` to limit the vocabulary size to the most frequent `vocab_size` words, handling out-of-vocabulary words by ignoring them or using a special token.

Now we construct our RNN model:

```python
embedding_dim = 128
```

```
model = Sequential([
Embedding(vocab size, embedding dim, input length=max length),
LSTM(128),
Dense(1, activation='sigmoid')
])
```

```python
model.compile(optimizer='adam',
loss='binary_crossentropy',
metrics=['accuracy'])

model.summary()
```

This defines a sequential model with an embedding layer to convert word indices into dense vectors, followed by an LSTM layer to capture sequential information, and finally a dense layer with a sigmoid activation function for binary classification (positive or negative). The model is compiled using the Adam optimizer and binary cross-entropy loss function, suitable for binary classification problems. `model.summary()` displays the model architecture and parameters.

Finally, we train the model:

```python
model.fit(padded *sequences, train labels,* epochs=10, batch_size=32)
```

This trains the model for 10 epochs with a batch size of 32. The number of epochs and batch size can be adjusted based on computational resources and performance. After training, we can evaluate the model's performance on the test set. Remember to preprocess the test data using the same tokenizer and padding as the training data.

```python
```

Assume 'test data' and 'test labels' are loaded from the IMDB dataset

```
test sequences = tokenizer.texts to sequences(test data)
padded test sequences = pad sequences(test sequences, maxlen=max_length)
loss, accuracy = model.evaluate(padded test sequences, test_labels)
print(f"Test Loss: {loss:.4f}")
print(f"Test Accuracy: {accuracy:.4f}")
```

This code evaluates the model on the test set and prints the loss and accuracy. A higher accuracy indicates better performance.

This example provides a basic framework. To enhance the model, consider adding techniques such as dropout regularization to prevent overfitting, experimenting with different LSTM layer sizes and hyperparameters, employing bidirectional LSTMs to process sequences in both directions for capturing more context, using different word embeddings (Word2Vec, GloVe), and implementing more advanced preprocessing techniques to refine the dataset. Furthermore, exploring different architectures like GRUs (Gated Recurrent Units) could yield improvements. Remember to carefully analyze the results and fine-tune the model based on your specific dataset and requirements. Properly addressing issues like overfitting and ensuring that the dataset is representative are essential steps in building a robust and accurate text classification model. This hands-on project serves as a foundation for more complex applications of RNNs and provides valuable experience in building and deploying deep learning models for natural language processing. The journey of building and refining this model underscores the iterative and experimental nature of machine learning development – a continuous process of refinement based on evaluation and analysis. Understanding and mastering these techniques are key to successfully applying AI to real-world problems. Furthermore, continued learning and exploring state-of-the-art techniques is essential to remaining current with the ever-evolving landscape of AI.

Applications of RNNs in NLP

Building upon our understanding of RNNs and LSTMs, we now delve into their diverse applications within the realm of Natural Language Processing (NLP). NLP, the field focused on enabling computers to understand, interpret, and generate human language, presents unique challenges and opportunities for RNNs. Their ability to process sequential data makes them particularly well-suited for tasks where the order of information is crucial, such as those found in NLP.

One of the most impactful applications of RNNs in NLP is **machine translation**
. Machine translation aims to
automatically convert text from one language to another. Traditional methods relied on rule-based systems and statistical approaches, but RNNs, particularly LSTMs and GRUs, have revolutionized the field. These models can learn complex relationships between words and phrases in different languages, capturing nuances that were previously difficult to handle. The input sequence is the source language text, and the output sequence is the target language translation. The model learns to map the source language sequence to the target language sequence through training on massive parallel corpora of translated text. The effectiveness of this approach stems from the RNN's ability to maintain context throughout the translation process, ensuring that the meaning is preserved accurately. Advanced techniques like attention mechanisms further enhance performance by allowing the model to focus on specific parts of the source sentence when generating the translation, improving fluency and accuracy. Furthermore, the use of encoder-decoder architectures, where one RNN encodes the source language and another decodes it into the target language, has significantly improved the quality of machine translation

systems. The ongoing research in this area focuses on handling rare words, improving fluency and accuracy, and dealing with low-resource languages where large parallel corpora are unavailable.

Another crucial application of RNNs in NLP is **sentiment analysis**. Sentiment analysis, also known as opinion mining, aims to determine the emotional tone expressed in a piece of text. This can be positive, negative, or neutral. RNNs excel at this task because they can capture the context and nuances expressed throughout a sentence or document. A simple sentiment analysis model might use an RNN to process the text and output a probability score for each sentiment category. For example, a model could predict the probability of a sentence expressing positive, negative, or neutral sentiment. More sophisticated models might employ multiple RNN layers or incorporate other techniques like attention mechanisms to improve accuracy. Sentiment analysis finds broad application in various domains, including customer feedback analysis, social media monitoring, brand reputation management, and market research. Analyzing customer reviews to gauge product satisfaction or monitoring social media to understand public opinion about a brand are just two examples of how sentiment analysis powered by RNNs is transforming businesses. Challenges in sentiment analysis include handling sarcasm, irony, and negation, which can often contradict the literal meaning of words. Ongoing research addresses these challenges by developing more robust models that can capture context and implicit meaning better.

Text generation is another area where RNNs have demonstrated remarkable capabilities. RNNs can learn to generate text that is coherent and stylistically similar to the input training data. This capability has applications in creative writing, chatbots, and even code generation. For text generation, an RNN is typically trained on a large corpus of text, learning the statistical relationships between words and sequences of words. Once trained, the model can be prompted with a starting sentence or phrase and generate subsequent text. The model generates text by predicting the next word in the sequence based on the previous words, iteratively extending the sequence until a specified length or termination condition is met. The quality of the generated text depends on the size and quality of the training data, as well as the architecture and hyperparameters of the RNN. While early models often produced nonsensical or repetitive text, recent advancements, particularly in the use of LSTMs and attention mechanisms, have resulted in significantly improved coherence and creativity. Examples include generating poems, articles, scripts, and even programming code. However, ethical considerations concerning the potential misuse of text generation technology, such as the creation of deepfakes or the spread of misinformation, need careful consideration.

Beyond these core applications, RNNs are used in a wide range of other NLP tasks. These include:

Named Entity Recognition (NER):
Identifying and classifying named entities in text, such as people,
organizations, locations, and dates. RNNs can capture the contextual information needed to correctly identify these entities.

Part-of-Speech (POS) Tagging:
Assigning grammatical tags to words in a sentence, such as noun, verb, adjective, adverb, etc. RNNs can learn the sequential dependencies between words to make accurate POS tagging decisions.

Question Answering:
Answering questions based on a given text passage. RNNs can be used to process both the

question and the text passage to identify the relevant information needed to answer the question.

Text Summarization:
Generating concise summaries of longer texts. RNNs can process the entire text and generate a shorter version that captures the essential information.

Dialogue Systems:
Building conversational agents or chatbots. RNNs can model the sequence of turns in a dialogue and generate appropriate responses.

The versatility of RNNs in NLP stems from their ability to handle sequential data and capture long-range dependencies. However, training RNNs, especially LSTMs, can be computationally expensive, and they can suffer from the vanishing gradient problem. Techniques like GRUs and attention mechanisms have mitigated some of these challenges, leading to significant improvements in performance and efficiency. The ongoing research in this field explores alternative architectures, such as Transformers, which have shown to outperform RNNs on many NLP tasks. Nevertheless, RNNs remain a crucial tool in the NLP toolkit, providing a powerful framework for tackling a wide range of challenging problems.

Furthermore, the successful implementation of RNNs in NLP often relies heavily on pre-processing techniques. These techniques aim to transform the raw text data into a format suitable for the model. Common preprocessing steps include:

Tokenization:
Breaking down the text into individual words or sub-word units.

Lowercasing:
Converting all text to lowercase to reduce the vocabulary size and avoid case sensitivity issues.

Stop word removal:
Removing common words that do not carry much meaning, such as "the," "a," "is," and "are."

Stemming or lemmatization:
Reducing words to their root form to improve model generalization.

Word embedding:
Representing words as dense vectors that capture semantic relationships between words. Techniques like Word2Vec and GloVe are commonly used for this purpose.

The careful application of these pre-processing steps can significantly impact the performance of an RNN model, improving accuracy and efficiency. Choosing appropriate pre-processing techniques depends on the specific NLP task and the characteristics of the data.

In conclusion, Recurrent Neural Networks have profoundly impacted the field of Natural Language Processing, providing effective solutions for a wide range of tasks. From machine translation and sentiment analysis to text generation and more, their ability to process sequential data and capture context has revolutionized how we interact with and interpret human language through computational means. While advancements continue to refine and improve these techniques, RNNs remain an essential component of the modern NLP toolkit, showcasing the power of deep learning in unlocking the complexities of human language. The continued research and development in this area promise even more impressive advancements in the years to come, pushing the boundaries of what's possible in human-computer interaction and understanding. As we move forward, it's crucial to remember the ethical implications associated with these powerful technologies and to employ them responsibly and thoughtfully.

The Transformer Architecture

The transformer architecture represents a significant advancement in deep learning, particularly in the realm of natural language processing (NLP). Unlike recurrent neural networks (RNNs), which process sequential data sequentially, transformers process the entire input sequence in parallel, leading to significant speed improvements and the ability to handle longer sequences more effectively. This parallel processing is achieved through the ingenious mechanism of self-attention.

At the heart of the transformer lies the self-attention mechanism. This mechanism allows the model to weigh the importance of different words in the input sequence when processing each word. Imagine reading a sentence: "The cat sat on the mat." A traditional RNN would process "The" first, then "cat," then "sat," and so on. In contrast, self-attention allows the model to consider the relationship between all words simultaneously. For instance, when processing "cat," the model can directly assess its relationship to "sat" and "mat," understanding that "cat" is the subject performing the action of "sitting" on the "mat." This simultaneous consideration of all word relationships provides a richer contextual understanding.

The self-attention mechanism is implemented using three matrices: query (Q), key (K), and value (V). These matrices are derived from the input embedding using linear transformations. For each word, its corresponding query vector is compared to the key vectors of all other words using a dot product. The result of this dot product is then scaled down (typically by the square root of the dimension of the key vectors) to prevent the values from becoming too large, which can hinder training. A softmax function is then applied to these scaled dot products, converting them into probabilities that represent the attention weights. Finally, these attention weights are multiplied by the value vectors, resulting in a weighted sum that represents the context-aware representation of each word.

This process, described above for a single word, is repeated for all words in the input sequence. The result is a set of context-aware representations where each word's representation incorporates information from all other words in the sequence, weighted by their relevance. This is a crucial difference from RNNs, which only consider the preceding words in the sequence.

To further enhance the model's ability to capture different aspects of the relationships between words, the transformer employs multi-head attention. Instead of using a single set of Q, K, and V matrices, multi-head attention uses multiple sets, each learning to focus on different relationships between words. The outputs of these multiple attention heads are then concatenated and linearly transformed to produce the final representation. This allows the model to capture more nuanced relationships and improve its overall performance.

Another key component of the transformer architecture is positional encoding. Since transformers process the input sequence in parallel, they lack inherent information about the order of words. Positional encoding addresses this by adding information about the position of each word in the sequence to its embedding. This can be done using various methods, such as sinusoidal functions or learned embeddings. The choice of positional encoding method can impact the model's performance, and research continues to explore optimal strategies.

The typical transformer architecture is built using an encoder-decoder structure. The encoder processes the input sequence, creating a contextualized representation of the input. This representation is then used by the decoder to generate the output sequence. In machine translation, for instance, the encoder processes the source sentence (e.g., in English), and the decoder generates the target sentence (e.g., in French). Each encoder and decoder layer typically consists of a multi-head self-attention layer followed by a feed-forward neural network. Residual connections and layer normalization are also commonly employed to improve training stability and performance.

The feed-forward network in each layer applies the same transformation to every position, but allows for different parameters for each position. This provides non-linearity to the model. Layer normalization helps stabilize the training process by normalizing the activations of each layer, preventing them from becoming too large or too small. Residual connections allow the gradient to flow more easily through the network, preventing vanishing gradients that can hinder training deep networks.

The transformer architecture has had a profound impact on the field of NLP. Its ability to process sequences in parallel and capture rich contextual information has led to significant improvements in various NLP tasks, such as machine translation, text summarization, question answering, and text generation. Models like BERT, GPT-3, and LaMDA, which are based on the transformer architecture, have demonstrated state-of-the-art performance on a wide range of benchmarks.

Beyond NLP, the transformer architecture is finding applications in other domains as well. Vision transformers (ViTs) have demonstrated impressive results in image classification and object detection tasks, challenging the dominance of convolutional neural networks. The adaptability and power of the transformer architecture suggest that its influence will continue to expand across many areas of deep learning.

The success of transformers is partly attributed to its scalability. The parallel processing nature allows for training significantly larger models with more parameters than previously feasible with RNNs. This scalability allows for the learning of more complex patterns and representations, leading to improved performance. Moreover, the relatively simple architecture, compared to some RNN variations, makes it easier to train and implement efficiently. However, the computational cost of training large transformer models remains substantial, requiring significant computing resources.

Further research is actively exploring various modifications and extensions of the basic transformer architecture. These include advancements in attention mechanisms, such as sparse attention to reduce computational complexity, and improvements in positional encoding to better handle long sequences. Efficient training techniques are also constantly being refined to handle the demands of ever-larger models. The development of more efficient architectures, combined with continuous advancements in hardware, will continue to push the boundaries of what's possible with transformers.

Furthermore, the inherent flexibility of the transformer architecture allows for integration with other deep learning techniques. For example, transformers can be combined with convolutional neural networks to leverage the strengths of both architectures for tasks involving both sequential and spatial data. This hybrid approach allows for a richer representation of complex data and can lead to improved performance. Similarly, combining transformers with reinforcement learning opens up possibilities for creating more intelligent and adaptive agents.

In conclusion, the transformer architecture represents a powerful and versatile tool for deep learning, particularly in the realm of natural language processing. Its parallel processing capabilities, self-attention mechanism, and encoder-decoder structure have led to significant advancements in various NLP tasks. The continuing research and development in this field promise even more groundbreaking applications in the future, pushing the boundaries of AI capabilities across a wide range of domains. The scalability and adaptability of the architecture ensures its continued relevance and impact on the field of AI for years to come. Its influence extends beyond NLP, making it a fundamental building block for numerous advanced AI systems. The simplicity of the core concepts, coupled with its immense power, makes it a compelling area of study for anyone interested in the forefront of artificial intelligence.

SelfAttention and MultiHead Attention

The core innovation of the Transformer architecture lies in its attention mechanism, specifically self-attention and its multi-headed variant. Understanding these mechanisms is crucial to grasping the power and efficiency of Transformers. Let's delve into the intricacies of self-attention. Imagine we have a sentence: "The quick brown fox jumps over the lazy dog." Traditional RNNs would process this sentence word by word, sequentially. However, self-attention allows the model to consider the relationship between *all* words simultaneously, regardless of their position in the sequence.

Self-attention works by assigning a weight to each word in the input sequence, representing its importance relative to every other word in the context of the current word being processed. This is achieved through three learned matrices: Query (Q), Key (K), and Value (V). These matrices are derived from the input word embeddings using linear transformations. For each word, its embedding is multiplied by the respective weight matrix (W_Q, W_K, W_V) to generate its query, key, and value vectors.

The query vector represents what the word is "looking for" in the context of other words. The key vector represents what the word "offers" to the context. The value vector represents the information the word contributes to the overall representation. The attention weight for a word pair is calculated by taking the dot product of the query vector of one word and the key vector of another word. This dot product measures the similarity between the two words. This score is then scaled down by the square root of the dimension of the key vectors ($\sqrt{d_k}$) to prevent the dot products from becoming too large, which can lead to instability during training. A softmax function is then applied to these scaled dot products to normalize them into probabilities, ensuring they sum to one. These probabilities represent the attention weights, indicating the importance of each word in the context of the current word.

Finally, these attention weights are used to weight the value vectors. The weighted sum of value vectors, calculated by multiplying each value vector by its corresponding attention weight, produces the context vector for the current word. This context vector incorporates information from all other words in the sequence, weighted by their relevance to the current word. This process is repeated for each word in the input sequence, resulting in a new set of representations that capture the relationships between all words in the sentence.

Let's illustrate this with a simple example. Consider the sentence: "The cat sat on the mat." For the word "cat," the self-attention mechanism might assign high weights to "sat" and "mat," as these words are closely related to "cat" in the sentence's context. Conversely, the weight for "the" might be lower, indicating a less significant relationship. The resulting context vector for "cat" would thus be a weighted combination of the value vectors for "cat," "sat," and "mat," capturing the semantic relationships within the sentence.

The mathematical representation clarifies this process. Given an input sequence $X = [x_1, x_2, ..., x_n]$, where each x_i is a word embedding, the self-attention mechanism can be expressed as:

$$\text{Attention}(Q, K, V) = \text{softmax}(QK^T/\sqrt{d_k})V$$

where Q, K, and V are the matrices of query, key, and value vectors, respectively. The output is a matrix of context vectors, one for each word in the input sequence.

While self-attention is powerful, multi-head attention takes this concept further. Instead of using a single set of Q, K, and V matrices, multi-head attention uses multiple sets, each learning different aspects of the input sequence. This allows the model to capture a richer understanding of the relationships between words, considering different types of relationships simultaneously. Each set of Q, K, and V matrices learns to focus on different aspects of the input sequence. For instance, one head might focus on syntactic relationships, while another might focus on semantic relationships.

The output of each head is then concatenated and linearly transformed to produce the final output. The number of heads (h) is a hyperparameter, typically set to 8 or 12. The use of multiple heads allows for parallelization, making the computation more efficient, while also enhancing the model's capacity to capture complex relationships.

The mathematical formulation of multi-head attention is:

$$\text{MultiHead}(Q, K, V) = \text{Concat}(\text{head}_1, \ldots, \text{head}_h)W^O$$

where $\text{head}_i = \text{Attention}(QW_i^Q, KW_i^K,$

W_i^K, W_i^V) and W_i^Q, W_i^K, W_i^V are the weight matrices for the i-th head, and W^O is a final output weight matrix.

The advantages of multi-head attention are significant. It allows the model to attend to different parts of the input sequence simultaneously and capture diverse relationships between words. This improves the model's ability to understand context, leading to improved performance on various NLP tasks. Furthermore, the parallel computation offered by multiple heads accelerates training and inference.

In practice, the self-attention and multi-head attention mechanisms are incorporated into the transformer architecture's encoder and decoder layers. The encoder uses self-attention to process the input sequence and generate contextualized representations. The decoder utilizes both self-attention (to attend to its own outputs) and encoder-decoder attention (to attend to the encoder's output) to generate the output sequence. This intricate interplay of attention mechanisms is what makes the transformer architecture so effective in handling long-range dependencies and complex relationships within sequential data. This parallel processing capacity, absent in RNNs, is a major reason for the Transformer's superior performance on tasks involving lengthy sequences. The ability to attend to all parts of the input sequence simultaneously allows the model to efficiently capture the context crucial for tasks like machine translation and text summarization.

The choice of the number of heads is a hyperparameter that needs careful tuning, balancing the computational cost with the potential increase in model accuracy. Too few heads might limit the model's ability to capture the complexity of the data, while too many heads can increase computational complexity without a commensurate increase in performance. Empirical studies have shown that increasing the number of heads often leads to performance gains up to a certain point, beyond which the gains diminish and the computational overhead becomes prohibitive. This optimal number depends on the dataset, the task, and the overall architecture of the Transformer model.

Beyond the core concepts, further refinements and extensions of the attention mechanism continue to be developed. These include techniques to improve efficiency, such as sparse attention mechanisms that reduce the computational cost of attending to all word pairs in long sequences. Other variations include relative positional encodings to incorporate positional information in the attention mechanism and hierarchical attention mechanisms to process information at multiple levels of granularity. The ongoing research and development in attention mechanisms are continuously pushing the boundaries of what's possible in the realm of deep learning and NLP. The versatility of the attention mechanism makes it applicable to various domains beyond NLP, including computer vision and time-series analysis, further highlighting its significance in the broader landscape of artificial intelligence. Its adaptability and effectiveness are key factors driving its continued prominence in the field.

Positional Encoding

The brilliance of the Transformer architecture lies in its ability to process sequential data, such as sentences or time series, by considering all elements simultaneously through the attention mechanism. However, this inherent parallelism presents a challenge: the attention mechanism, in its raw form, is position-agnostic. It treats all input tokens equally, regardless of their order. This is problematic because the meaning of a sentence fundamentally depends on the order of words. "The dog bit the man" conveys a very different meaning than "The man bit the dog." To address this critical limitation, Transformer models employ positional encoding.

Positional encoding is a crucial technique that adds information about the position of each word in the input sequence. This allows the model to understand not only the relationships between words but also their order within the sequence. Several methods exist for implementing positional encoding, each with its strengths and weaknesses. Let's explore some of the most common approaches.

One straightforward approach is to use absolute positional embeddings. In this method, each position in the input sequence is assigned a unique vector representing its position. These vectors are learned during the training process, similar to word embeddings. The advantage of this method is its simplicity; it directly incorporates positional information into the input representation. However, this approach has limitations. The model's ability to handle sequences longer than those seen during training is hampered. If it encounters a sequence length beyond its training data, it can struggle to generalize effectively because it hasn't learned embeddings for those new positions.

Furthermore, the model may struggle to extrapolate to positions far beyond what it has been exposed to during training. Essentially, the model is memorizing positional information rather than learning a general representation of position.

To overcome the limitations of absolute positional embeddings, relative positional encoding offers a more flexible solution. Instead of assigning fixed vectors to each position, relative positional encoding focuses on the relative distances between words. This means the model learns to represent the relationship between a word and its neighbors, regardless of their absolute positions. This approach allows for better generalization to longer sequences because the model is learning a more abstract concept of position rather than a specific positional index. One common implementation uses sinusoidal functions to generate positional encodings. These functions are defined as:

$$PE(pos, 2i) = \sin(pos / 10000^{(2i/d_{model})})$$

$$PE(pos, 2i+1) = \cos(pos / 10000^{(2i/d_{model})})$$

where:

`pos` is the position of the word in the sequence.
`i` is the dimension index.
`d_model` is the embedding dimension.

These sinusoidal functions create a rich representation of positional information, allowing the model to capture both absolute and relative positions. The use of different frequencies allows the model to differentiate between different distances. This is crucial because close words usually have a stronger relationship than those far apart.

Another significant advantage of sinusoidal positional encoding is that it can extrapolate to positions beyond those seen during training. Since the functions are defined mathematically, they can generate encodings for any position, allowing the model to handle sequences of arbitrary lengths. This makes it a robust and scalable solution. The model doesn't need to memorize specific positions, and thus, is less prone to overfitting on the training data. The model learns to discern positional relationships from the inherent properties of these functions, allowing the generalization capabilities to extend to longer sequences than previously observed.

Let's contrast this with the learned absolute positional embeddings. These embeddings are typically learned during training, and they might be only as good as the training data. If the longest sequence in the training data is 100 words, the model might struggle to understand positional relationships in a sentence with 1000 words. The sinusoidal approach, however, doesn't suffer from this limitation. It's a more general, mathematically defined encoding that can handle longer sequences effectively.

However, sinusoidal positional encoding isn't without its drawbacks. While it handles long sequences well, it lacks the expressiveness of learned embeddings. The learned embeddings can capture nuanced relationships between position and other features that might not be captured by the sinusoidal function. This means there's a tradeoff between the ability to generalize and the richness of the learned positional representation.

A hybrid approach combines the strengths of both learned embeddings and sinusoidal functions. This could involve learning small adjustments to the sinusoidal encodings, which allows the model to fine-tune the positional representation based on the specific training data while maintaining the generalization capabilities of sinusoidal encoding.

Another avenue of research explores incorporating positional information directly into the attention mechanism itself. This approach, known as relative positional attention, modifies the attention calculation to explicitly consider the relative positions of words. This avoids the need for separate positional encoding vectors, but it introduces complexity into the attention mechanism itself.

Regardless of the chosen method, the incorporation of positional information is crucial for Transformer models to understand sequential data effectively. The choice between absolute, relative, or hybrid encoding techniques depends on the specific task, dataset, and computational resources available. Careful consideration of these factors is essential to optimize the model's performance.

The impact of positional encoding extends far beyond the basic understanding of word order. It is particularly crucial for tasks involving long-range dependencies. In tasks like machine translation, where the relationship between words at the beginning and end of a sentence is crucial, positional encoding is essential to capture these distant relationships. Imagine translating a sentence like "The book that was written by the renowned author and published last year is finally available." The relationship between "book" and "available" requires capturing a long-range dependency that wouldn't be possible without positional information.

Furthermore, positional encoding's influence extends to other domains beyond NLP. In time series analysis, understanding the temporal ordering of data points is paramount. For example, in financial modeling, predicting future stock prices relies on understanding the historical sequence of prices. Positional encoding plays a vital role in enabling Transformer-based models to accurately model these time-dependent relationships. Similarly, in computer vision, positional information is crucial for tasks like object detection and image captioning where understanding the spatial arrangement of objects within an image is paramount. In these contexts, positional encoding can take the form of spatial embeddings, indicating the x and y coordinates of image features.

The ongoing research on positional encoding focuses on developing more efficient and expressive methods that can handle increasingly complex and lengthy sequences. Techniques like sparse attention and hierarchical attention are being combined with advanced positional encoding schemes to improve the scalability and performance of Transformer models, particularly for very long sequences where computational cost becomes a significant bottleneck. The search for optimal positional encoding methods is an active area of research that will continue to shape the future development of Transformer models and their applications in various fields. The ability to effectively capture positional information is not simply an ancillary feature but a foundational aspect that significantly influences the power and effectiveness of the Transformer architecture. As we delve further into the nuances of AI and its applications, understanding these underlying mechanisms becomes ever more critical.

EncoderDecoder Structure

The core of many successful Transformer models lies in their elegant encoder-decoder structure. This architecture, inspired by the sequence-to-sequence models that preceded them, provides a powerful framework for tackling tasks involving the transformation of one sequence into another. Think of machine translation, where an input sequence in English needs to be converted into an output sequence in French. Or consider text summarization, where a long input document needs to be condensed into a shorter, coherent summary. The encoder-decoder structure is perfectly suited to these kinds of tasks.

The encoder's role is to process the input sequence and transform it into a contextualized representation, a rich encoding that captures the meaning and relationships between the input elements. This encoding is not simply a linear transformation of the input; rather, it's a sophisticated representation that leverages the attention mechanism to capture long-range dependencies within the sequence. Each input token is not processed in isolation, but in the context of all other tokens, allowing the model to understand the nuanced relationships between words and phrases. For example, in the sentence "The quick brown fox jumps over the lazy dog," the encoder will not only understand the individual meaning of each word, but also the relationships between "quick" and "fox," "jumps" and "over," and "lazy" and "dog," capturing the overall meaning and structure of the sentence. This contextualized representation is crucial for subsequent processing stages.

The encoder's architecture typically consists of multiple identical layers, each composed of two sub-layers: a multi-head self-attention layer and a feed-forward neural network. The self-attention mechanism, as discussed previously, allows the model to attend to different parts of the input sequence simultaneously, weighting the importance of each token based on its relationship to other tokens. This allows the model to capture long-range dependencies that would be difficult to handle with recurrent neural networks (RNNs) due to their sequential processing nature. The feed-forward network further processes the output of the self-attention layer, adding another level of transformation and non-linearity to the representation. Each layer operates on the output of the previous layer, progressively refining the contextualized representation. The output of the final encoder layer serves as the input to the decoder.

The decoder's primary function is to generate the output sequence based on the contextualized representation produced by the encoder. It also employs a layered architecture similar to the encoder, utilizing self-attention and feed-forward networks. However, the decoder incorporates a crucial addition: encoder-decoder attention. This mechanism allows the decoder to attend not only to the previously generated output tokens (self-attention) but also to the entire encoded input sequence. This interaction between the encoder and decoder is fundamental to the Transformer's ability to map the input sequence to the output sequence effectively. The encoder-decoder attention mechanism allows the model to focus on the relevant parts of the input while generating each output token. For instance, in machine translation, when generating a French word, the decoder can attend to the corresponding English words in the input sentence to ensure accurate translation.

Let's consider a practical example of machine translation. The input sentence is "The cat sat on the mat." The encoder processes this sentence, generating a contextualized representation that captures the relationships between words. This representation is then fed to the decoder. The decoder, using encoder-decoder attention, can access this representation to generate the French translation, word by word. As the decoder generates each word ("Le," "chat," "s'est," "assis," "sur," "le," "tapis"), it uses encoder-decoder attention to focus on the relevant parts of the English sentence to ensure the accuracy of the translation. The self-attention within the decoder ensures that the generated words are contextually coherent with each other. This interplay between self-attention and encoder-decoder attention is what gives Transformer models their power.

The interaction between the encoder and decoder is not a one-way street. Information flows in both directions. The encoder provides a rich representation of the input, guiding the decoder's generation process. Conversely, the decoder's generation process, through the encoder-decoder attention mechanism, indirectly influences the encoder's representation, leading to a more refined and accurate overall processing. This dynamic interaction between the encoder and decoder is a significant factor in the effectiveness of the Transformer architecture.

The depth of both the encoder and decoder is a hyperparameter that can be tuned to suit the complexity of the task. Deeper models, with more layers, are typically capable of learning more complex relationships between input and output sequences. However, increasing the depth also increases the computational cost and the risk of overfitting. Finding the optimal depth requires careful experimentation and validation on the specific dataset and task.

Furthermore, the implementation details of the encoder and decoder, such as the number of attention heads, the hidden layer dimensions in the feed-forward networks, and the specific activation functions, all play a role in the performance of the Transformer model. These choices often involve careful experimentation and are guided by both theoretical considerations and empirical observations. The field is constantly evolving, and new techniques and variations of the basic encoder-decoder structure are continually being explored and refined.

Beyond machine translation and text summarization, the encoder-decoder structure has proven remarkably versatile and applicable to a wide array of sequence-to-sequence tasks. In speech recognition, for instance, the encoder processes the audio input, converting it into a sequence of phonetic units, while the decoder generates the corresponding text transcription. Similarly, in image captioning, the encoder processes the visual information from an image, generating a contextualized representation, and the decoder generates a descriptive caption for the image. The adaptability of the encoder-decoder structure highlights its significance in the broader field of AI and its remarkable ability to solve complex problems involving sequential data.

The efficiency of the encoder-decoder architecture is also a significant advantage. The inherent parallelism of the attention mechanism allows for efficient processing of long sequences, overcoming the limitations of sequential models like RNNs that suffer from vanishing gradients and slow training times with long sequences. This parallelism is a crucial factor in the scalability of Transformer models, allowing them to handle the large datasets often encountered in real-world applications.

The development of the encoder-decoder architecture represents a significant step forward in AI. It combines the power of attention mechanisms with a modular and adaptable design, allowing for efficient and effective processing of sequential data in a wide range of tasks. While the architecture has been refined and improved upon since its inception, its fundamental design remains highly influential and continues to serve as the basis for many of the most advanced language models and AI systems currently available. Understanding its workings is fundamental to understanding the capabilities and limitations of modern AI.

Furthermore, researchers continually explore variations and improvements to the encoder-decoder framework. For example, the introduction of different attention mechanisms, such as sparse attention or hierarchical attention, aims to address the computational limitations associated with processing extremely long sequences. These innovations demonstrate the ongoing evolution of the architecture and its enduring significance in the landscape of AI research and development. The exploration of novel techniques for efficient attention and enhanced contextual representation is an active area of research, promising even more powerful and versatile Transformer models in the future. The quest for better, more efficient, and scalable AI models relies heavily on advancements in this fundamental architectural structure. The core concepts of encoding and decoding, coupled with the power of attention, remain central to the pursuit of increasingly intelligent systems. The continued exploration and refinement of this architecture will undoubtedly shape the future trajectory of AI.

Applications of Transformers in NLP and Beyond

The power of the Transformer architecture extends far beyond the theoretical elegance of its design. Its impact is profoundly felt across a vast spectrum of natural language processing (NLP) tasks and is increasingly making inroads into other domains. This versatility stems from its ability to effectively capture long-range dependencies within sequential data, a feat that eluded previous architectures. Let's delve into some key applications:

One of the most celebrated successes of Transformers is in **machine translation**
. Before Transformers, recurrent neural networks (RNNs), particularly LSTMs and GRUs, were the dominant approach. However, RNNs struggle with long sequences due to the vanishing gradient problem.
Transformers, with their parallel processing capability through the self-attention mechanism, elegantly overcome this limitation. Models like Google's Transformer, and subsequent iterations such as the Transformer-XL and the BERT-based models, have achieved state-of-the-art results in translating between multiple language pairs, often surpassing human performance in certain benchmarks. The ability to process entire sentences simultaneously allows for a richer understanding of context, leading to more accurate and
fluent translations. This has significantly impacted global communication, facilitating cross-cultural understanding and access to information across language barriers. Furthermore, the efficiency gains offered by Transformers have enabled real-time translation applications, impacting fields like international business, diplomacy, and tourism.

Another significant application lies in
text summarization
. Extracting the key information from lengthy documents is a

crucial task with implications across various domains, from news aggregation to legal document review. Transformers excel at this by leveraging their ability to understand the contextual relationships between different parts of a text. Models can be trained to generate concise summaries that accurately reflect the main points of the original document, preserving its meaning and intent. Different summarization techniques, including abstractive and extractive summarization, can be implemented using Transformers, offering flexibility depending on the desired output. Abstractive summarization, where the model generates new sentences to summarize the text, often requires more sophisticated models capable of capturing nuanced meanings. This technology has profound implications for improving information access, accelerating research, and enhancing productivity across numerous professions.

Beyond summarization, Transformers are revolutionizing **question answering systems**. These systems aim to provide accurate and relevant answers to questions posed in natural language. Transformers' capacity to understand intricate relationships within text allows them to identify the relevant parts of a document that contain the answer to a given question. This is particularly valuable for tasks involving complex reasoning, where understanding the context and relationships between different pieces of information is crucial. Models like BERT and RoBERTa have demonstrated remarkable performance on question answering benchmarks, pushing the boundaries of what's achievable in this field. The development of robust question answering systems holds immense potential for improving access to information, powering more intelligent search engines, and facilitating knowledge discovery.

Sentiment analysis, the task of determining the emotional tone of a piece of text, is another area where Transformers have demonstrated significant impact. Traditional methods often rely on simpler techniques like counting the frequency of positive and negative words. However, Transformers can capture much more nuanced sentiment by considering the context in which words are used. This allows for a more accurate assessment of the overall sentiment, even when dealing with sarcasm or irony, which can be challenging for simpler methods. The applications of sentiment analysis are widespread, ranging from social media monitoring to market research and customer service analysis. Understanding customer sentiment can inform product development, marketing strategies, and overall business decisions. The improved accuracy offered by Transformer-based models is crucial for making informed decisions based on large amounts of textual data.

The power of Transformers extends beyond text. Their ability to handle sequential data has led to applications in **image captioning**
. In this task, the model generates a descriptive caption for an image, effectively bridging the gap between visual and textual information. Transformers can achieve this by learning to associate visual features extracted from the image with relevant words and phrases. This necessitates a combined approach integrating computer vision techniques (like CNNs) with Transformer architectures. The resultant models can generate captions that are both accurate and descriptive, making them valuable for indexing and retrieving images, as well as creating alternative text descriptions for accessibility purposes.

Furthermore, Transformers are finding applications in areas beyond NLP, including
time series forecasting
, a field crucial for predicting future trends in various domains. The ability of Transformers to capture long-range dependencies is particularly advantageous in analyzing time series data, where correlations between data points can span extended

periods. Applications range from predicting stock prices and energy consumption to weather forecasting and traffic flow optimization. The power of Transformers lies in their ability to effectively learn complex patterns within the data, providing more accurate and reliable predictions.

The field of **bioinformatics** has also benefited from the advancements brought about by Transformers. The analysis of biological sequences, such as DNA and proteins, involves dealing with long sequences of data, making it a natural fit for Transformer-based models. These models are being used to predict protein structure, identify genes, and understand the complex interactions within biological systems. This has far-reaching implications for drug discovery, disease diagnosis, and personalized medicine.

Moreover, Transformers are increasingly used in **speech recognition** and **speech synthesis**. In speech recognition, the sequential nature of audio signals makes Transformers a powerful tool for accurate transcription. Similarly, in speech synthesis, Transformers can be used to generate highly natural-sounding speech from text, offering significant advancements in areas like voice assistants and accessibility tools.

In conclusion, the Transformer architecture is more than just an advancement in NLP; it represents a paradigm shift in the way we approach sequential data processing. Its versatility and effectiveness have led to a plethora of applications, and ongoing research continues to unveil new possibilities. The flexibility of the architecture, combined with the ever-increasing computational power available, suggests that Transformers will play an increasingly crucial role in shaping the future of artificial intelligence across a variety of disciplines. The ongoing development of more efficient and powerful Transformer models promises even greater

advancements in the years to come, expanding their influence into areas we can only begin to imagine. The fundamental principles of attention and parallel processing remain at the core of this transformative technology, driving innovation and pushing the boundaries of what's possible in the field of AI. From enhancing communication to
revolutionizing healthcare, the impact of Transformers is undeniable and will continue to grow exponentially. The future looks bright, indeed, for this remarkable architecture.

Introduction to Reinforcement Learning Concepts

Reinforcement learning (RL) stands apart from supervised and unsupervised learning paradigms. Instead of learning from explicitly labeled data or discovering patterns in unlabeled data, RL focuses on an agent learning to interact with an environment to maximize cumulative rewards. Imagine a robot learning to navigate a maze: it doesn't have pre-defined instructions for each step, but instead learns through trial and error, receiving positive rewards for reaching the goal and negative rewards for hitting obstacles. This trial-and-error process, guided by rewards, is the essence of reinforcement learning.

At the heart of RL are four fundamental concepts: agents, environments, rewards, and policies. The
agent
is the learner and decision-maker, the entity trying to solve the problem.
This could be anything from a simple algorithm to a complex robot or even a software program. The
environment is everything the agent interacts with. It's the space in which the agent operates and receives feedback. In the maze
example, the environment is the maze itself, including the walls, the goal, and any other obstacles.

The
reward
is a numerical signal the environment sends to the agent after each action. Rewards guide the learning process; positive rewards incentivize actions that lead
towards the desired goal, while negative rewards penalize undesirable actions. In the maze navigation example, a positive reward might be given upon reaching the goal, while negative rewards could be given for hitting walls. The crucial aspect here is that the reward signal is usually

delayed; the agent doesn't receive immediate feedback for every action. For instance, in a complex game, a winning action might only yield a reward after a series of intermediate steps. This delayed reward characteristic presents significant challenges in designing effective RL algorithms.

The *policy* is a strategy or mapping that dictates the agent's actions based on the current state of the environment. It's the agent's decision-making mechanism. A policy can be deterministic (always choosing the same action in the same state) or stochastic (choosing actions probabilistically). Learning an optimal policy, that is, a policy that maximizes the cumulative reward over time, is the ultimate goal of reinforcement learning.

The interaction between the agent and the environment unfolds as a sequence of states, actions, and rewards. The agent starts in an initial state, selects an action according to its current policy, and the environment transitions to a new state, giving the agent a reward reflecting the outcome of that action. This cycle continues until the agent reaches a terminal state (like solving the maze or completing a game) or a pre-defined number of steps is reached. The agent's objective is to learn a policy that maximizes its expected cumulative reward over this sequence of interactions.

Different RL problems have varying characteristics, influencing the design and choice of algorithms. The most important of these characteristics is the *Markov property*. A problem satisfies the Markov property if the future state depends only on the current state and the chosen action, and not on the previous history of states and actions. This simplifies the problem significantly, as the agent only needs to consider the current state when making decisions. Many RL problems are modeled as Markov Decision Processes (MDPs), a mathematical framework explicitly incorporating the Markov property. MDPs provide a formal structure for defining and solving RL problems, allowing for theoretical analysis and algorithm design.

A key distinction in RL is between model-based and model-free approaches. In *model-based RL*, the agent explicitly learns a model of the environment; this model predicts the next state and reward given the current state and action. This model allows the agent to plan its actions, simulating future interactions and choosing actions that optimize long-term rewards. In contrast, *model-free RL* does not explicitly learn a model of the environment; instead, it learns the optimal policy directly from experience through trial and error.
Model-free approaches are often simpler to implement but can be less efficient in terms of sample complexity, requiring many interactions with the environment to learn a good policy.

The choice between model-based and model-free methods depends on the specific problem and available resources. Model-based methods can be more sample efficient, needing fewer interactions to learn a good policy, but they require more computational resources for building and maintaining the environment model. Model-free methods can be more robust to model misspecifications, as they don't rely on an accurate model of the environment.

Several algorithms fall under the umbrella of reinforcement learning. Q-learning, a model-free algorithm, is a fundamental technique. It works by learning a Q-function, which estimates the expected cumulative reward starting from a given state and taking a given action. The Q-function is updated iteratively through the Bellman equation, a recursive relationship that expresses the value of a state-action pair in terms of the rewards and values of future states. Q-learning is relatively simple to understand and implement, making it a good starting point for learning RL.

Deep Q-Networks (DQNs) extend Q-learning by incorporating deep neural networks to approximate the Q-function. This allows the algorithm to handle high-dimensional state spaces, a common challenge in complex RL problems. DQNs use deep learning's power to represent complex functions and learn from large amounts of data. The use of neural networks significantly increases the algorithm's capacity to solve problems with many states and actions, opening possibilities for applications in complex domains like robotics and game playing. However, DQNs are more computationally expensive than traditional Q-learning and require careful consideration of hyperparameters and network architecture for optimal performance.

Policy gradient methods represent another significant class of RL algorithms. Instead of directly learning a Q-function, these methods learn the policy directly by optimizing it to maximize the expected cumulative reward. This involves updating the policy parameters using gradient ascent, a technique that iteratively adjusts the parameters to increase the expected reward. Policy gradient methods can be very effective in continuous action spaces, where Q-learning can struggle. They also naturally handle stochastic policies, providing flexibility in the decision-making process.

Beyond the core algorithms, many advanced techniques have been developed to address specific challenges in RL. These include techniques for dealing with partial observability (where the agent doesn't have access to the complete state), hierarchical reinforcement learning (where tasks are decomposed into subtasks), and multi-agent reinforcement learning (where multiple agents interact and learn within the same environment). These advanced techniques are essential for tackling the complexity of real-world problems.

In summary, reinforcement learning provides a powerful framework for building agents that can learn to interact with their environments and achieve complex goals. The concepts of agents, environments, rewards, and policies, along with the various algorithms and techniques, offer a rich toolkit for designing intelligent systems. The choice of algorithm depends on the specific characteristics of the problem, including the complexity of the state and action spaces, the presence or absence of a model, and the desired level of control over the agent's actions. As we progress, understanding these nuances will become crucial in effectively applying reinforcement learning in diverse and challenging settings.

QLearning Algorithm

Q-learning, a model-free reinforcement learning algorithm, stands as a cornerstone of the field. Unlike model-based methods that require explicit knowledge of the environment's dynamics (transition probabilities and reward functions), Q-learning learns directly from experience, making it particularly adaptable to complex and uncertain environments. Its core idea revolves around estimating a Q-function, which represents the expected cumulative reward an agent can obtain by taking a specific action in a given state and subsequently following an optimal policy.

The Q-function, denoted as Q(s, a), maps a state-action pair (s, a) to a scalar value representing the estimated future reward. The goal of Q-learning is to learn the optimal Q-function, denoted as Q
(s, a), which provides the maximum expected cumulative reward for each state-action pair. Once this optimal Q-function is learned, the agent can simply select the action that maximizes Q
(s, a) for the current state to follow an optimal policy.

The learning process in Q-learning is iterative, relying on the Bellman equation, a fundamental concept in dynamic programming. The Bellman equation states that the optimal Q-value for a state-action pair is the immediate reward received plus the discounted maximum expected future reward achievable from the subsequent state. Mathematically, this is expressed as:

$$Q(s, a) = R(s, a) + \gamma \max_{a'} Q(s', a')$$

where:

R(s, a) is the immediate reward received after taking action 'a' in state 's'.

γ (gamma) is the discount factor, a value between 0 and 1 that determines the importance of future rewards (a lower gamma prioritizes immediate rewards).

s' is the next state reached after taking action 'a' in state 's'.

$\max_{a'} Q(s', a')$ represents the maximum Q-value among all possible actions in the next state s'.

The Q-learning algorithm updates the Q-function iteratively using the following update rule:

$$Q(s, a) \leftarrow Q(s, a) + \alpha [R(s, a) + \gamma \max_{a'} Q(s', a') - Q(s, a)]$$

where:

α (alpha) is the learning rate, a value between 0 and 1 that controls the step size of the updates. A smaller alpha leads to slower but potentially more stable learning, while a larger alpha can lead to faster but potentially more unstable learning.

Let's illustrate Q-learning with a simple example: a grid world. Imagine a 4x4 grid where the agent starts at a specific location (e.g., the top-left corner). The goal is to reach a designated target cell (e.g., the bottom-right corner), and the agent can move up, down, left, or right in each step. Moving into the target cell yields a reward of +1, hitting a wall results in a reward of -1, and all other moves have a reward of 0. We'll use a discount factor (γ) of 0.9 and a learning rate (α) of 0.1.

Initially, the Q-values for all state-action pairs are initialized to 0. The agent begins exploring the grid randomly, selecting actions based on an exploration strategy (e.g., ε-greedy, where the agent selects a random action with probability ε and the action with the highest Q-value with probability $1-\varepsilon$). After each action, the agent observes the reward and the new state. The Q-value for the state-action pair corresponding to the previous state and action is updated using the Q-learning update rule.

For instance, suppose the agent is in state (1,1) and takes action 'right', moving to state (1,2). Let's assume it receives a reward of 0. The Q-value update would be:

$$Q(1,1, \text{right}) \leftarrow Q(1,1, \text{right}) + 0.1 [0 + 0.9 \max_{a'} Q(1,2, a') - Q(1,1, \text{right})]$$

This process continues as the agent explores the grid. Over time, the Q-values converge towards the optimal Q-values, allowing the agent to learn a policy that maximizes its cumulative reward. The exploration strategy is crucial; purely exploiting the current best policy may prevent the agent from discovering potentially better alternatives. The ε-greedy approach offers a balance between exploration and exploitation.

The convergence of Q-learning is theoretically guaranteed under certain conditions, primarily requiring the exploration strategy to ensure that all state-action pairs are visited infinitely often. However, in practice, convergence can be slow, especially in large state spaces. The choice of learning rate (α) and discount factor (γ) significantly impacts the learning process. Choosing appropriate values for these parameters is crucial for efficient learning and avoiding oscillations or slow convergence. Too small an alpha may lead to slow learning, while too large an alpha may cause instability. Similarly, the discount factor determines the balance between immediate and long-term rewards. A small discount factor prioritizes immediate rewards, whereas a large discount factor emphasizes long-term rewards.

Furthermore, Q-learning's effectiveness can be significantly impacted by the size of the state and action spaces. In large, continuous spaces, the Q-function becomes challenging to represent and update efficiently. This limitation has motivated the development of Deep Q-Networks (DQNs), which utilize deep neural networks to approximate the Q-function, enabling the application of Q-learning to high-dimensional problems. DQNs address the curse of dimensionality by using function approximation, allowing the learning algorithm to handle problems with vast state and action spaces, far exceeding the capabilities of traditional tabular Q-learning.

Beyond the core algorithm, several variations and extensions of Q-learning exist to address specific challenges. For example, Double Q-learning mitigates the overestimation bias inherent in the standard Q-learning update rule. SARSA (State-Action-Reward-State-Action), another on-policy algorithm, updates Q-values based on the action actually taken in the next state, providing a different learning perspective compared to the off-policy nature of Q-learning.

In conclusion, Q-learning provides a powerful and versatile framework for solving reinforcement learning problems. Its model-free nature, reliance on the Bellman equation, and iterative update rule make it remarkably adaptable to various environments. While challenges exist, particularly in high-dimensional spaces, the development of DQN and other extensions has significantly broadened the applicability and practical impact of Q-learning across diverse domains. Understanding the nuances of Q-learning—the impact of learning rate, discount factor, exploration strategies, and potential biases—is vital for effectively leveraging its power in building intelligent agents capable of mastering complex tasks. This algorithm remains a pivotal building block in the arsenal of reinforcement learning techniques. Its elegance and effectiveness continue to drive significant advancements in the field of artificial intelligence.

Deep QNetworks DQNs

Deep Q-Networks (DQNs) represent a significant advancement over traditional Q-learning, particularly when dealing with complex environments and high-dimensional state spaces. The limitations of traditional Q-learning become apparent when confronted with problems involving a vast number of states and actions. The Q-table, used to store the Q-values (expected cumulative rewards), grows exponentially with the number of states and actions, leading to the curse of dimensionality. This makes it computationally infeasible and memory-intensive to maintain and update the Q-table effectively. Furthermore, the discrete nature of the Q-table restricts its application to environments with discrete state and action spaces. Continuous state spaces, common in many real-world problems, require sophisticated discretization techniques, which can lead to significant information loss and reduced accuracy.

DQNs elegantly circumvent these limitations by employing a deep neural network to approximate the Q-function. Instead of explicitly storing Q-values in a table, a DQN learns to map state-action pairs to their corresponding Q-values through the network's weights. This allows for a compact and efficient representation of the Q-function, even in high-dimensional spaces. The network's ability to generalize from limited experiences means that it can estimate Q-values for unseen state-action pairs, significantly improving the algorithm's robustness and applicability.

The architecture of a typical DQN consists of several fully connected layers, each with a non-linear activation function (such as ReLU), followed by an output layer that produces Q-values for each possible action in the given state. The input to the network is typically a vector representation of the current state. For image-based environments, convolutional layers are often incorporated at the beginning of the network to extract relevant features from the image data. The network's weights are adjusted using a process similar to that used in supervised learning, but with a crucial difference: the target values are derived from the reinforcement learning process, specifically the Bellman equation.

Training a DQN involves an iterative process where the agent interacts with the environment, collects experience (state, action, reward, next state tuples), and uses this experience to update the network's weights. A key component of DQN training is the use of experience replay. Experience replay involves storing the agent's experiences in a memory buffer and randomly sampling batches of experiences from this buffer during training. This helps to break the temporal correlations between consecutive experiences, which can lead to instability during training. By sampling randomly, the network is exposed to a more diverse set of experiences, leading to better generalization and more stable learning.

Another crucial aspect of DQN training is the use of a target network. The target network is a copy of the main network that is updated periodically (e.g., every few thousand steps). Using a target network helps to stabilize the training process by providing a more stable target for the Q-value updates. Without a target network, the updates can become highly correlated, leading to oscillations or divergence. The target network acts as a more stable estimate of the Q-values, reducing the impact of changing weights on the update target.

The training process involves minimizing a loss function, typically the mean squared error (MSE) between the predicted Q-values from the main network and the target Q-values from the target network. This loss function is minimized using gradient descent, a common optimization algorithm used in deep learning. The gradients are calculated using backpropagation, which propagates the error back through the network's layers, allowing the network to adjust its weights accordingly. Hyperparameter tuning, including the choice of learning rate, discount factor, and experience replay buffer size, plays a crucial role in the success of DQN training.

Compared to traditional Q-learning, DQNs offer several significant advantages. Their ability to handle high-dimensional state spaces makes them applicable to a much wider range of problems. The use of function approximation enables generalization to unseen states and actions, improving robustness and efficiency. Furthermore, the experience replay mechanism and target network help to stabilize the training process, making it more likely to converge to a good solution. However, DQNs also present challenges. The training process can be computationally intensive, requiring substantial computing resources. Careful hyperparameter tuning is necessary to achieve optimal performance, and the choice of network architecture can significantly influence the results.

Let's consider a practical example to illustrate the power of DQNs. Imagine training an agent to play the Atari game Breakout. In this game, the state space is complex, consisting of the entire game screen (a high-dimensional image). Using traditional Q-learning would be computationally infeasible due to the vast number of possible states. However, a DQN can effectively learn to play this game by using convolutional layers to extract relevant features from the game screen and then using fully connected layers to map these features to Q-values for each possible action (e.g., moving the paddle left, right, or not moving). The experience replay and target network mechanisms help to stabilize the training process, enabling the DQN agent to learn a successful strategy. The agent will start by exploring random actions but gradually learn to prioritize actions that lead to higher scores, improving its performance over time.

Another compelling application of DQNs lies in robotics. Consider the task of teaching a robot arm to manipulate objects. The state space here consists of the robot arm's configuration, the position and orientation of the objects, and potentially other sensory information. This is a high-dimensional continuous space that would be extremely difficult to handle with traditional Q-learning. However, a DQN can be used to approximate the Q-function, enabling the robot to learn a policy for manipulating objects effectively. The DQN can be trained using simulated environments or real-world data, providing a flexible and powerful approach to robotic control.

The success of DQNs has spurred significant research into further improvements and extensions. Double DQN (DDQN) addresses the overestimation bias inherent in standard DQNs by using two separate networks – one to select actions and another to evaluate their Q-values. Dueling DQN further refines this approach by decomposing the Q-function into two components: a state-value function (representing the value of being in a particular state) and an advantage function (representing the advantage of taking a specific action in a given state). This decomposition can improve the stability and efficiency of the learning process. Prioritized experience replay gives priority to experiences that are more informative, allowing the network to focus on the most important updates. These and other advancements continue to expand the capabilities and applicability of DQNs across diverse domains.

In summary, Deep Q-Networks have revolutionized reinforcement learning, providing a powerful and efficient method for solving complex problems involving high-dimensional state and action spaces. While challenges remain, the ongoing research and development in this area promise to further extend the reach and impact of DQNs in various applications, from gaming and robotics to resource management and financial modeling. The combination of deep learning and reinforcement learning methodologies presents a truly powerful framework for building intelligent agents capable of mastering complex and dynamic environments. Understanding DQNs, their architecture, and training process, is essential for any serious student of AI and its applications in the modern world. The core concepts—experience replay, target networks, and the interplay
between deep learning and reinforcement learning paradigms—represent fundamental building blocks in the evolving landscape of artificial intelligence.

Building a Simple GamePlaying AI

Let's move beyond the theoretical underpinnings of Deep Q-Networks and build something tangible: a game-playing AI. While we could tackle a complex game like Go or StarCraft, a simpler environment allows us to focus on the core principles without getting bogged down in intricate game mechanics. We'll create an AI agent that learns to play a simplified version of a classic game – a deterministic grid-world environment. This environment, though basic, encapsulates the key elements of reinforcement learning: states, actions, rewards, and the agent's learning process.

Our game will consist of a grid, say 5x5, where the agent, represented by a symbol (e.g., 'A'), starts at a specific location. The goal is to reach a target location (e.g., 'G') within a set number of steps. The agent can move up, down, left, or right, one cell at a time. Moving into the target cell yields a positive reward (e.g., +10), while each step taken consumes a small amount of reward (e.g., -1). Hitting a wall results in no movement and no reward penalty. This creates a clear objective and a structured environment where our agent can learn optimal paths.

The state space in this game is straightforward. Each cell on the grid represents a unique state. If we have a 5x5 grid, our state space consists of 25 possible states. The action space is equally simple: up, down, left, and right, four discrete actions. This simplicity contrasts with the complexities of games like chess or Go, where the state and action spaces are exponentially larger, making traditional Q-learning approaches impractical. However, even this small game will showcase the power of reinforcement learning.

We'll implement our agent using Python and a few key libraries. NumPy provides efficient array operations necessary for handling our Q-table. We'll use Matplotlib for visualization, allowing us to see the agent's learning progress. Let's get started with the code. First, we need to define our environment:

```python
import numpy as np
import matplotlib.pyplot as plt
import random

class GridWorld:
    def __init__(self, size=5):
        self.size = size
        self.grid = np.zeros((size, size))
        self.agent_pos = (0, 0)  # Initial agent position
        self.goal_pos = (size - 1, size - 1)  # Goal position
        self.walls = []  # You can add walls later if you want to make it more complex

    def reset(self):
        self.agent_pos = (0, 0)
        return self.agent_pos

    def step(self, action):
        x, y = self.agent_pos
        if action == 0:  # Up
            x = max(0, x - 1)
        elif action == 1:  # Down
            x = min(self.size - 1, x + 1)
        elif action == 2:  # Left
            y = max(0, y - 1)
        elif action == 3:  # Right
            y = min(self.size - 1, y + 1)
```

```
self.agent_pos = (x, y)
reward = -1  Reward for each step
done = self.agent
```
pos == self.goal
```
pos  Check if goal is reached
return self.agent_pos, reward, done
```
```

This `GridWorld` class sets up our game. We define the grid size, agent starting position, and goal position. The `step` method takes an action (0-3) as input, updates the agent's position, and returns the new position, reward, and a boolean indicating if the goal has been reached. The `reset` method resets the agent to its starting position. We could easily extend this class to add obstacles or more complex reward structures.

Now, let's implement the Q-learning algorithm itself. Remember, our state space is small enough for a simple Q-table:

```python
class QLearningAgent:
def
```
init
```
(self, env, learning
```
rate=0.1, discount
```
factor=0.9, exploration_rate=0.1):
self.env = env
self.learning
```
rate = learning
```
rate
self.discount
```
factor = discount
```
factor
self.exploration
```
rate = exploration
```
rate
self.q_table = np.zeros((env.size, env.size, 4))  4 actions
```
```

```python
def choose_action(self, state):
    if random.uniform(0, 1) < self.exploration_rate:
        return random.randint(0, 3)  Explore randomly
    else:
        return np.argmax(self.q_table[state[0], state[1]])  Exploit best action
```

```python
def learn(self, state, action, reward, next_state, done):
    old_value = self.q_table[state[0], state[1], action]
    next_max = np.max(self.q_table[next_state[0], next_state[1]])
    new_value = (1 - self.learning_rate) * old_value + self.learning_rate * (reward + self.discount_factor * next_max)
    self.q_table[state[0], state[1], action] = new_value

def train(self, num_episodes):
    for episode in range(num_episodes):
        state = self.env.reset()
        done = False
        while not done:
            action = self.choose_action(state)
            next_state, reward, done = self.env.step(action)
            self.learn(state, action, reward, next_state, done)
            state = next_state

        if (episode + 1) % 100 == 0:
            print(f"Episode {episode+1}/{num_episodes} completed.")
```

The `QLearningAgent` class initializes with parameters for the learning rate, discount factor, and exploration rate. The `choose_action` method uses an epsilon-greedy strategy, balancing exploration and exploitation. The `learn` method updates the Q-values using the Q-learning update rule. The `train` method runs the training loop for a specified number of episodes.

Finally, let's put it all together and train our agent:

```python
env = GridWorld()
agent = QLearningAgent(env)
```

```
agent.train(num_episodes=5000)

Visualize the learned Q-values
plt.imshow(np.max(agent.q_table, axis=2))
plt.colorbar()
plt.show()

Test the agent
state = env.reset()
done = False
while not done:
action = agent.choose_action(state)
next_state, reward, done = env.step(action)
print(f"Agent moved from {state} to {next_state} with reward {reward}")
state = next_state
```

This code creates a `GridWorld` environment, an agent using Q-learning, trains the agent, and then tests its performance. The visualization shows the learned Q-values, highlighting the optimal paths learned by the agent. You can experiment with different learning rates, discount factors, and exploration rates to observe their effects on the agent's learning process.

This example demonstrates a basic game-playing AI using Q-learning. While simple, it illustrates the fundamental concepts of reinforcement learning in a clear and concise way. The simplicity allows us to focus on the core algorithm and its interaction with the environment, paving the way for understanding more complex applications of reinforcement learning. Further refinements could involve adding obstacles, multiple goals, stochasticity (introducing randomness into the environment), or even expanding to a larger grid. All of these extensions can be incorporated using the foundation we've built here, highlighting the flexibility and adaptability of this framework. Remember to install the necessary libraries (`numpy`, `matplotlib`) before running this code. The visualization provides a visual representation of the learned policy, showing the agent's preferred actions in different states. Observe how the values gradually converge as the agent learns the optimal strategy for reaching the goal. This simple exercise lays a solid groundwork for tackling more complex reinforcement learning tasks in the future. This project provides a practical stepping stone to more advanced topics like Deep Q-Networks, which we've previously discussed, and other cutting-edge reinforcement learning techniques.

Advanced Reinforcement Learning Techniques

Building upon our understanding of Q-learning and Deep Q-Networks (DQNs), we now delve into more sophisticated reinforcement learning techniques. While Q-learning and its deep learning counterpart provide effective solutions for many problems, their limitations become apparent when dealing with complex environments or continuous action spaces. These limitations stem from the reliance on estimating the Q-function, which can be computationally expensive and prone to instability, especially in high-dimensional state spaces. This necessitates exploring alternative approaches that offer improved efficiency and stability. Two prominent families of methods address these challenges: policy gradients and actor-critic methods.

Policy gradient methods, unlike Q-learning, directly optimize the policy—the agent's strategy for selecting actions in different states. Instead of estimating the value function, policy gradient methods aim to maximize the expected cumulative reward by directly adjusting the policy's parameters. This approach bypasses the need for explicitly estimating the Q-function, potentially leading to better performance and stability, especially in continuous action spaces. A key advantage of policy gradients is their ability to handle stochastic policies, allowing the agent to explore the environment more effectively. This is in contrast to Q-learning, which often relies on epsilon-greedy exploration, a strategy that can become less efficient in complex scenarios.

One common policy gradient method is REINFORCE (Reinforcement Learning with Monte Carlo Estimation), a relatively straightforward algorithm. REINFORCE uses Monte Carlo simulations to estimate the gradient of the expected cumulative reward with respect to the policy parameters. The gradient is then used to update the policy parameters using an optimization algorithm like stochastic gradient ascent. While conceptually simple, REINFORCE can suffer from high variance in its gradient estimates, leading to slow and unstable learning. This variance stems from the reliance on complete episodes for gradient estimation, amplifying the impact of random events.

To mitigate the high variance problem inherent in REINFORCE, several variance reduction techniques have been developed. One effective approach is to incorporate a baseline, which is a function that estimates the expected cumulative reward. Subtracting the baseline from the return (cumulative reward) reduces the variance of the gradient estimates without affecting the expected gradient. A common choice for the baseline is the average return over a set of episodes, which provides a reliable estimate of the expected reward.

Actor-critic methods represent a significant advancement over both vanilla policy gradients and Q-learning. These methods combine the strengths of both approaches, leveraging a policy (the actor) to select actions and a critic to evaluate the policy's performance. The actor learns to improve its policy by directly optimizing its parameters, while the critic learns to estimate the value function, providing feedback to guide the actor's learning. This synergy allows for more efficient and stable learning compared to either policy gradients or Q-learning alone.

The critic's role in actor-critic methods is crucial for several reasons. First, it provides a stable estimate of the value function, which can be used to guide the actor's policy updates. This is particularly beneficial in environments with sparse rewards, where the cumulative reward might be highly variable and noisy. Second, the critic helps reduce the variance of the policy gradient estimates, leading to more efficient learning. Finally, the critic can facilitate exploration by providing estimates of the value of different actions, allowing the actor to prioritize actions with higher expected returns.

There are various implementations of actor-critic methods, differing in how the actor and critic are parameterized and how their parameters are updated. One popular approach is using neural networks for both the actor and the critic, leading to deep actor-critic methods. In these methods, the actor network maps states to action probabilities, while the critic network estimates the value function for given state-action pairs. The parameters of both networks are updated using techniques such as temporal-difference learning (TD learning), a family of reinforcement learning algorithms which learn from incomplete episodes, thereby reducing variance compared to Monte Carlo methods. Several variations on TD learning exist, with SARSA (State-Action-Reward-State-Action) and Q-learning being notable examples.

A key advantage of deep actor-critic methods lies in their ability to handle high-dimensional state and action spaces, making them applicable to a wide range of complex problems. For example, they have been successfully applied to robotics control, game playing, and resource management. The flexibility in network architectures allows for adapting to different problem characteristics.

Another class of advanced techniques revolves around model-based reinforcement learning. Unlike model-free methods like Q-learning and policy gradients, which learn directly from experience, model-based methods learn a model of the environment's dynamics. This model predicts the next state and reward given the current state and action. This predicted model can then be used to plan actions, allowing for more efficient exploration and improved sample efficiency. The learned model can be used for planning via methods such as Monte Carlo Tree Search (MCTS), which evaluates different action sequences by simulating future interactions with the environment. Model-based methods can also be combined with model-free approaches, creating hybrid algorithms that benefit from both model-based planning and model-free learning.

The advantages of model-based methods are considerable. They often exhibit better sample efficiency, requiring fewer interactions with the actual environment to learn an optimal policy. This is because they can use their learned model to simulate many interactions without needing to actually execute them in the real environment. Furthermore, model-based methods can generalize better to unseen states and actions, as the learned model can extrapolate beyond the experienced data. However, the accuracy of the learned model is critical for the success of model-based methods. Inaccurate models can lead to poor planning and suboptimal policies.

Advanced techniques like Trust Region Policy Optimization (TRPO) and Proximal Policy Optimization (PPO) address the challenge of large policy updates, which can destabilize the learning process in policy gradient methods. These methods constrain the policy updates to ensure that the new policy doesn't deviate too much from the old policy, leading to more stable and efficient learning. TRPO employs a sophisticated mathematical framework to guarantee monotonic improvement, while PPO offers a simpler, more practical approach that maintains good performance.

Beyond these methods, other advanced techniques such as hierarchical reinforcement learning (decomposing complex tasks into subtasks) and transfer learning (leveraging knowledge gained from previous tasks to accelerate learning on new tasks) are actively being researched and developed. These approaches aim to tackle the challenges of scaling reinforcement learning to increasingly complex and diverse problems. Each of these methods offers unique advantages and limitations, and the choice of the most appropriate method depends heavily on the specific problem characteristics and available computational resources.

Finally, it's crucial to mention the ongoing research in areas like exploration strategies, reward shaping, and multi-agent reinforcement learning. Effective exploration remains a key challenge in reinforcement learning, and advanced strategies continue to be developed to ensure thorough exploration of the state-action space. Reward shaping techniques aim to improve learning efficiency by carefully designing the reward function, guiding the agent towards desirable behavior. Multi-agent reinforcement learning deals with the complexities of multiple agents interacting within the same environment, requiring coordination and negotiation to achieve collective goals. These ongoing advancements highlight the dynamic nature of the field and the continuous development of more sophisticated and powerful reinforcement learning algorithms. The development and application of these advanced techniques will undoubtedly lead to further breakthroughs in AI and its capabilities across diverse applications.

Text Preprocessing Techniques

Before we can effectively use text data for tasks like sentiment analysis, machine translation, or chatbot development, we need to transform it into a format that AI models can understand. This crucial step is known as text preprocessing, and it involves a series of techniques designed to clean, normalize, and structure the raw text data. This process significantly impacts the accuracy and performance of our NLP models. Neglecting proper preprocessing can lead to poor model performance and unreliable results.

One of the fundamental steps in text preprocessing is **tokenization**. This involves breaking down the raw text into individual units, typically words or sub-word units. A simple approach might involve splitting the text based on spaces. However, this simplistic method struggles with punctuation and complex linguistic structures. More sophisticated tokenizers utilize regular expressions or advanced algorithms to handle punctuation, contractions, and other complexities more effectively. For example, the sentence "Don't worry, be happy!" would be tokenized as ["Don't", "worry", ",", "be", "happy", "!"] using a space-based approach, but a more advanced tokenizer might produce ["Don't", "worry", ",", "be", "happy", "!"]. The choice of tokenizer can heavily influence subsequent processing and model performance. Libraries like NLTK and spaCy provide robust tokenization capabilities tailored to various languages.

Following tokenization, we often employ techniques to reduce words to their root forms, simplifying the vocabulary and improving model performance.
Stemming
is a rule-based approach that chops off word endings to obtain a stem.

While efficient, stemming can sometimes produce non-dictionary words, or "stems", that lack linguistic meaning. For example, stemming "running" might yield "run," while stemming "better" might produce "bett," which isn't a valid word.

Lemmatization
, a more sophisticated approach, uses vocabulary and morphological analysis to reduce words to their dictionary forms, or lemmas. Lemmatization considers the context of the word and aims to produce linguistically correct lemmas. This ensures that different forms of the same word (e.g., "run," "running," "ran") are all reduced to the same lemma ("run"). Lemmatization is generally preferred over stemming for its higher accuracy, although it is computationally more intensive. Tools like WordNet lemmatizer in NLTK provide powerful lemmatization capabilities. The choice between stemming and lemmatization depends on the specific application and the desired level of accuracy. For tasks where linguistic accuracy is critical, lemmatization is highly recommended. For computationally constrained environments, stemming could be a more practical option.

Beyond stemming and lemmatization, further preprocessing steps enhance the quality and usability of our text data.
Stop word removal
eliminates common words (e.g., "the," "a," "is," "are") that often carry little semantic meaning. These words can clutter the data and increase the computational burden without contributing significantly to model performance. However, removing stop words should be approached cautiously. Certain stop words might be crucial for specific tasks; for example, in sentiment analysis, the word "not" is a crucial negation word that alters the meaning of a sentence. Therefore, whether to remove stop words is highly task-dependent.

Handling punctuation
involves removing or replacing punctuation marks. While some punctuation can convey important information (e.g., exclamation marks indicating strong emotion), excessive punctuation can interfere with model training. A common approach involves removing punctuation entirely, but in some cases, specific punctuation might be retained or replaced with special tokens. Similarly, **handling numbers** requires decisions on how to represent numerical data. For some applications, numbers can be removed, while for others, they might be retained or
converted to a specific numerical representation.

Lowercasing
is a straightforward step that converts all text to lowercase. This eliminates the distinction between
uppercase and lowercase letters, which can be irrelevant for some NLP tasks. However, for certain applications that require capitalization sensitivity (e.g., Named Entity Recognition), lowercasing should be avoided.

Cleaning noisy text
addresses issues such as misspellings, typos, and irrelevant characters. Techniques like spell
checking and regular expression-based cleaning can improve data quality. For example, removing HTML tags or unnecessary whitespace is crucial if the text data originates from web sources.

The choice of preprocessing techniques is often task-dependent. For example, sentiment analysis might benefit from stop word removal and lemmatization, whereas machine translation might require more careful handling of punctuation and number representation. Experimentation and evaluation are key to determining the optimal preprocessing pipeline for a particular NLP task. The impact of preprocessing should be rigorously evaluated using appropriate metrics like accuracy, precision, and recall to ensure that the chosen steps improve model performance.

Consider the example of analyzing customer reviews for a product. Raw reviews contain various forms of the same word (e.g., "good," "better," "best"), punctuation, stop words, and numbers. Tokenization breaks down the reviews into individual words. Lemmatization reduces these words to their base forms ("good," "good," "good"). Stop word removal eliminates common words. Finally, the cleaned data is suitable for sentiment analysis. Without preprocessing, the model would struggle to identify the underlying sentiment accurately. The model would be overwhelmed by irrelevant data and might fail to discern the underlying sentiment effectively.

Another illustration focuses on building a chatbot. In this case, effective text preprocessing is vital for the chatbot to understand user input correctly. The raw user input, typically filled with typos, slang, and informal language, requires cleaning and normalization. Tokenization separates the input into meaningful units. Stemming or lemmatization reduces words to their root forms. The preprocessed input helps the chatbot find the best response in the dataset. Without effective preprocessing, the chatbot might fail to understand the user's intent, leading to unsatisfactory interactions. In essence, a chatbot relies on consistent and meaningful parsing of the user's input; proper preprocessing facilitates this process.

Advanced preprocessing techniques also exist, including techniques to handle negation, handling contractions more effectively, handling rare words (often through methods like replacing with an "unknown" token or applying specific techniques for out-of-vocabulary words) and normalization for different text formats like dates, times, and URLs. These techniques can dramatically improve the accuracy and robustness of the downstream NLP model. The choice of the most appropriate techniques, however, heavily relies on the specific data and the intended application. Experimentation, careful evaluation, and iterative refinement are essential for developing a text preprocessing pipeline that optimizes the performance of any NLP model. The efficiency and accuracy of the NLP pipeline are significantly determined by the quality and thoroughness of the preprocessing stage. It is a non-trivial process that demands careful consideration of the nuances of the chosen language and the specific task at hand. In conclusion, while seemingly a minor step, robust text preprocessing forms the cornerstone of effective Natural Language Processing.

WordVec and GloVe

Having prepared our text data through meticulous preprocessing, we now arrive at a critical juncture in our NLP journey: representing words in a way that machines can understand and utilize effectively. Raw text, as we've seen, is essentially a sequence of characters and words, a format ill-suited for direct consumption by most machine learning models. This is where word embeddings come into play. Word embeddings are dense, low-dimensional vector representations of words, capturing semantic and syntactic relationships between them. Instead of representing a word as a discrete symbol, we map it to a continuous vector space, where similar words have vectors that are closer together. This allows us to leverage the power of vector algebra to perform various NLP tasks efficiently.

Imagine words like "king," "queen," "man," and "woman." In a traditional representation, these would be completely separate, distinct entities. But semantically, they share strong relationships. A word embedding would capture these relationships, placing the vectors for "king" and "queen" closer together, and similarly for "man" and "woman." Furthermore, the vector difference between "king" and "man" might be surprisingly similar to the vector difference between "queen" and "woman," reflecting the analogous gender relationships. This ability to capture relationships is crucial for NLP tasks because it allows the model to understand the nuances of language and perform inferences it could not otherwise manage.

Two prominent techniques for generating word embeddings are Word2Vec and GloVe. Let's delve into the details of each.

Word2Vec

Word2Vec, developed by Google, is a powerful and widely used technique for learning word embeddings. It leverages neural networks to learn vector representations of words from a large corpus of text. The core idea is to train a neural network to predict the context of a word given the word itself, or vice versa. Word2Vec offers two main architectures: Continuous Bag-of-Words (CBOW) and Skip-gram.

In CBOW, the model tries to predict a target word given its surrounding context words. The context is essentially a "bag" of words, where the order of words doesn't matter. The model takes the context words as input, averages their vector representations, and then uses a neural network to predict the target word. The model learns vector representations for words in such a way that similar words have similar vector representations.

The Skip-gram architecture takes a different approach. Here, the model tries to predict the surrounding context words given a target word. This is often considered more effective in capturing long-range dependencies between words and identifying subtle semantic nuances. Imagine the sentence "The quick brown fox jumps over the lazy dog." In the skip-gram model, given the word "fox," the model would try to predict words like "quick," "brown," "jumps," and "over," capturing the contextual relationships. The model is trained to maximize the probability of observing these context words given the target word.

The training process for both CBOW and Skip-gram involves iterating through the training corpus, feeding word and context pairs to the neural network. Backpropagation adjusts the weights of the network, refining the word vector representations iteratively. Once training is complete, the resulting word vectors are the learned embeddings, which can then be used in other NLP tasks.

One of the key advantages of Word2Vec is its relative simplicity and efficiency. It's relatively straightforward to implement and train, even with large datasets. Its performance, while impressive, is not without limitations. It struggles with rare words and out-of-vocabulary (OOV) words, which often lack sufficient contextual information for accurate vector representation. Furthermore, Word2Vec captures only the word-level co-occurrence statistics and doesn't explicitly model more complex syntactic and semantic phenomena.

GloVe (Global Vectors for Word Representation)

GloVe, another prominent technique for learning word embeddings, adopts a different approach that leverages global word-word co-occurrence statistics. Instead of directly training a neural network on word-context pairs, GloVe uses a matrix factorization method to learn word vectors. It builds a co-occurrence matrix, where each entry (i, j) represents the number of times word i appears in the context of word j. This matrix provides a global perspective on word relationships.

The core idea behind GloVe is to learn vector representations that capture the ratios of co-occurrence probabilities. The model essentially learns to predict these ratios accurately.
For instance, the ratio of the co-occurrence probability of "ice" and "solid" compared to the co-occurrence probability of "ice" and "steam" can provide information about the semantic similarity between "solid" and "steam" in relation to "ice." This global perspective often leads to more robust and accurate embeddings.

GloVe utilizes matrix factorization techniques, often employing least squares regression, to find the word vectors that minimize the difference between predicted and observed co-occurrence probability ratios. This optimization process yields a set of word vectors that capture both local and global contextual information.

One significant advantage of GloVe is its ability to effectively handle rare words and OOV words compared to Word2Vec. Because it leverages global co-occurrence statistics, even infrequent words might still have sufficient information to generate reasonably accurate vector representations. This makes GloVe more robust when dealing with diverse and potentially sparse datasets. Additionally, GloVe often shows improved performance in tasks like analogy solving, where subtle semantic relationships are crucial.

However, GloVe's increased performance comes at the cost of potentially increased computational resources and complexity. Building and factorizing the co-occurrence matrix can be computationally intensive, particularly for large corpora.

Choosing between Word2Vec and GloVe

The choice between Word2Vec and GloVe often depends on the specific application and the characteristics of the data.
Word2Vec, with its relative simplicity and efficiency, is a great starting point for many NLP tasks. Its performance is often quite satisfactory. GloVe, on the other hand, often exhibits superior performance in scenarios requiring capturing more subtle semantic relationships or handling rare words effectively. The computational overhead of GloVe should be considered, particularly for very large datasets. In practice, experimenting with both methods and evaluating

their performance on a specific dataset is the best way to determine which technique provides optimal results. Recent advancements have also led to hybrid approaches that combine the strengths of both methods, yielding even better performance.

Beyond Word2Vec and GloVe, many other word embedding techniques have been developed, each with its own strengths and weaknesses. FastText, for example, extends the Word2Vec architecture to consider subword information, improving the handling of OOV words and morphologically rich languages. Contextualized embeddings, such as those produced by ELMo, BERT, and other transformer-based models, represent a significant advancement, capturing context-dependent representations of words, leading to state-of-the-art results in various NLP tasks. These contextualized embeddings, however, require significantly more computational resources for generation and usage. They represent a more advanced topic and will be discussed in later chapters.

The choice of word embedding technique is a crucial step in any NLP pipeline. The proper selection significantly impacts the downstream performance of your NLP models. Understanding the strengths and weaknesses of each approach, and carefully evaluating their performance on your specific dataset, is essential for building high-performing NLP applications. The field of word embeddings is constantly evolving, with new and improved techniques continuously emerging. Keeping abreast of the latest developments is vital for staying at the forefront of NLP innovation. This foundation in word embeddings will serve as a bedrock for the more advanced NLP techniques we will explore throughout the remainder of this book.

Recurrent Neural Networks for NLP

Building upon our understanding of word embeddings, we now turn our attention to recurrent neural networks (RNNs), a powerful class of neural networks specifically designed for processing sequential data. This makes them exceptionally well-suited for natural language processing (NLP) tasks, where the order of words significantly impacts meaning. Unlike feedforward neural networks, which process inputs independently, RNNs possess a "memory" that allows them to consider past inputs when processing current ones. This memory is implemented through loops in their architecture, enabling them to maintain a context across the sequence.

The fundamental building block of an RNN is a hidden state, often denoted as h. This hidden state is updated at each time step, incorporating information from the current input and the previous hidden state. The update rule typically involves a weighted sum of the current input, the previous hidden state, and a bias term, all passed through a non-linear activation function (e.g., tanh or sigmoid). This process can be mathematically represented as:

$$h_t = f(W_{xh} x_t + W_{hh}$$

$h_{t-1} + b_h)$

where:

h_t is the hidden state at time step t.

x_t is the input at time step t (e.g., a word embedding).

W_{xh} is the weight matrix connecting the input to the hidden state.

W_{hh} is the weight matrix connecting the previous hidden state to the current hidden state.

b_h is the bias vector.
f is the non-linear activation function.

This equation elegantly captures the essence of RNNs: the current hidden state is a function of both the current input and the past context encoded in the previous hidden state. The output of the RNN at each time step can be derived from the hidden state using another weight matrix and activation function. This allows the RNN to not only process sequential data but also to generate sequential outputs, making them suitable for tasks like machine translation and text generation.

However, standard RNNs suffer from a significant limitation: the vanishing gradient problem. During backpropagation through time (BPTT), the gradients used to update the weights can shrink exponentially as they propagate through long sequences. This makes it difficult for the RNN to learn long-range dependencies between words in a sentence, significantly hindering performance on tasks where context over extended spans is crucial.

Long Short-Term Memory (LSTM) networks were developed to address this issue. LSTMs introduce a more sophisticated cell state, denoted as c, which acts as a conveyor belt of information across the sequence. Instead of simply updating the hidden state, LSTMs use a carefully designed set of gates – input, output, and forget gates – to control the flow of information into and out of the cell state. These gates are themselves neural networks that learn to regulate the information flow, mitigating the vanishing gradient problem.

The gates operate as follows:

Forget Gate:
This gate decides what information to discard from the cell state. It takes the previous hidden state and the current input as inputs and outputs a value between 0 and 1, indicating the degree to which each component of the cell state should be forgotten.

Input Gate:
This gate determines what new information should be added to the cell state. It consists of two parts: one that generates a candidate vector for the new cell state, and another that decides which parts of this candidate vector to add to the cell state.

Output Gate:
This gate determines what parts of the cell state should be outputted as the hidden state. It takes the current cell state and the previous hidden state as inputs and outputs a value between 0 and 1, indicating which parts of the cell state to output.

The equations governing these gates and the cell state update are more complex than those of a standard RNN, but they effectively allow LSTMs to maintain and update information over much longer sequences. This enables LSTMs to capture long-range dependencies, significantly improving their performance on various NLP tasks.

Gated Recurrent Units (GRUs) represent another variant of RNNs designed to address the vanishing gradient problem. While similar in spirit to LSTMs, GRUs have a simpler architecture with fewer parameters. They combine the forget and input gates into a single update gate and merge the cell state and hidden state. This simplification can lead to faster training and reduced computational cost, making them a competitive alternative to LSTMs in many applications. However, the choice between LSTM and GRU often depends on the specific task and dataset; empirical evaluation is crucial for determining which architecture performs best.

The application of RNNs and their variants in NLP is remarkably diverse. Consider the following examples:

Sentiment Analysis:
RNNs can analyze text sequences to determine the overall sentiment (positive, negative, or neutral) expressed. The model processes the words
sequentially, capturing the context and nuances in the text that influence sentiment. For example, a sentence like "The movie was amazing, but the ending was disappointing" requires the model to consider both positive and negative aspects to arrive at a balanced sentiment score.

Machine Translation:
RNN-based sequence-to-sequence models, often employing LSTMs or GRUs, are widely used in machine translation. The encoder RNN processes the source sentence, producing a context vector that
encapsulates the meaning. The decoder RNN then uses this context vector to generate the translated sentence in the target language. The ability of RNNs to handle sequential data makes them exceptionally well-suited for this task.

Text Summarization:
Extractive or abstractive text
summarization techniques rely heavily on RNNs to process the input text and generate a concise summary. Extractive summarization involves selecting important sentences from the original text, while abstractive summarization involves generating a new summary that captures the essence of the original text.

Named Entity Recognition (NER):
RNNs can be used to identify and classify named entities in text, such as person names, organizations, locations, and dates. The model

processes the text sequentially, identifying patterns and contextual cues that help in identifying these entities.

Part-of-Speech (POS) Tagging:
RNNs can be effectively used to assign grammatical tags (e.g., noun, verb, adjective) to each word in a sentence. This task requires understanding the context in which a word appears to determine its correct POS tag.

Beyond these applications, RNNs and their advanced architectures are continuously being refined and adapted for an ever-expanding range of NLP tasks. Research into more efficient and robust RNN architectures, along with the development of novel training techniques, continues to drive improvements in the performance of these models.

However, it's crucial to acknowledge the limitations of RNNs. While LSTMs and GRUs significantly mitigate the vanishing gradient problem, they can still struggle with extremely long sequences. Furthermore, training RNNs can be computationally expensive, particularly for large datasets. This computational cost increases significantly with the length of sequences. This has fueled the development of alternative architectures such as Transformers, which possess a parallel processing capability allowing for efficient handling of long sequences and have demonstrated superior performance on many NLP tasks. Transformers are capable of capturing long-range dependencies more effectively than RNNs, and their parallel processing nature leads to faster training times. Despite this, RNNs remain a fundamental and valuable component within the broader NLP ecosystem. Understanding their strengths and limitations is vital for effectively employing these powerful tools within the realm of artificial intelligence. As we progress, understanding their underlying mechanics and limitations will enable us to make informed decisions in selecting the optimal architecture for our specific NLP project. The next chapter will delve into these alternative architectures, including the transformative impact of the Transformer model.

Transformers for NLP

The limitations of recurrent neural networks (RNNs), particularly their struggles with long sequences and computational cost, spurred the development of a revolutionary architecture: the Transformer. Unlike RNNs, which process sequences sequentially, Transformers leverage a mechanism called "self-attention" to process all parts of the input sequence simultaneously. This parallel processing capability dramatically accelerates training and allows for the effective capture of long-range dependencies within text, a crucial aspect often missed by RNNs.

The core innovation of the Transformer lies in its self-attention mechanism. This mechanism allows the model to weigh the importance of different words in the input sequence when processing each word. Instead of relying on a sequential processing chain like RNNs, self-attention allows the model to consider all words in the sequence concurrently, enabling it to identify relationships between words regardless of their distance in the sequence. This is a significant advantage over RNNs, which are hampered by the vanishing gradient problem when dealing with long-range dependencies. In essence, self-attention allows the model to understand the context of each word in relation to all other words, leading to a more nuanced and comprehensive understanding of the input text.

The self-attention mechanism works by calculating attention weights for each word pair in the input sequence. These weights represent the importance of each word in relation to every other word. The calculation involves three matrices: Query (Q), Key (K), and Value (V). These matrices are derived from the input embeddings through linear transformations. For each word, the query vector is compared to the key vectors of all other words using a dot product. The result is then scaled down and passed through a softmax function to obtain the attention weights. These weights are then used to weigh the value vectors, producing a context vector for each word, which encapsulates the information from all other words in the sequence. This context vector is then used as input for the next layer of the network.

The architecture of a Transformer typically consists of an encoder and a decoder. The encoder processes the input sequence and generates a contextualized representation, while the decoder generates the output sequence based on this representation. Both the encoder and decoder are composed of multiple stacked layers, each containing a self-attention layer and a feed-forward neural network. The self-attention layers allow the model to capture long-range dependencies within the input and output sequences, while the feed-forward networks further process the information. Residual connections and layer normalization are also incorporated to improve training stability and performance.

The Transformer's ability to process sequences in parallel and capture long-range dependencies has led to significant advancements in various NLP tasks. It has achieved state-of-the-art results in machine translation, text summarization, question answering, and many other areas. Several prominent Transformer-based models have emerged, including BERT (Bidirectional Encoder Representations from Transformers), GPT (Generative Pre-trained Transformer), and T5 (Text-to-Text Transfer Transformer).

BERT, a powerful bidirectional Transformer model, is pre-trained on a massive corpus of text data and is fine-tuned for specific downstream tasks. Its bidirectional nature allows it to consider both the preceding and following context when processing each word, providing a more comprehensive understanding of the text. BERT's pre-training on a large dataset allows it to learn rich representations of words and phrases, leading to improved performance on a wide range of NLP tasks.

GPT, on the other hand, is a unidirectional Transformer model, generating text sequentially. Its pre-training focuses on predicting the next word in a sequence, enabling it to learn the probabilistic relationships between words. This makes GPT particularly effective for text generation tasks, such as writing articles, generating code, and creating creative text formats. The successive models in the GPT series, especially GPT-3 and its successors, have showcased the remarkable capabilities of large language models in generating human-quality text.

T5, a text-to-text transfer Transformer model, frames all NLP tasks as text-to-text problems. This approach simplifies the training process and allows for the efficient use of a single model for various tasks. T5's consistent text-to-text formulation facilitates transfer learning, where knowledge learned from one task is transferred to another, leading to improved performance on diverse NLP applications.

The success of Transformer models is largely attributed to their ability to capture long-range dependencies and process sequences in parallel. This contrasts sharply with RNNs, which struggle with long sequences and are computationally expensive to train. The self-attention mechanism, the core of the Transformer architecture, is responsible for these improvements. By allowing the model to simultaneously consider all words in a sequence, self-attention enables a more comprehensive understanding of the context, leading to state-of-the-art performance on various NLP tasks.

However, Transformers are not without their limitations. Despite their parallel processing capabilities, they can still be computationally expensive, especially when dealing with very long sequences. Moreover, the large number of parameters in these models makes them resource-intensive to train and deploy. Research is ongoing to address these limitations, exploring techniques such as model compression and efficient training algorithms.

The development of Transformer models represents a major breakthrough in NLP. Their ability to effectively capture long-range dependencies and process sequences in parallel has revolutionized the field, leading to substantial advancements in various NLP applications. While challenges remain, ongoing research continues to refine and enhance these powerful models, promising further advancements in the years to come. Understanding the intricacies of the Transformer architecture and the self-attention mechanism is crucial for anyone seeking to develop cutting-edge NLP systems. The ability to leverage these models effectively unlocks a wide array of possibilities in diverse applications, from machine translation to chatbots and beyond. The journey of exploring the capabilities of Transformers is far from over, and continuous research and innovation will undoubtedly shape the future of Natural Language Processing. The ongoing development of more efficient training methods and the exploration of novel architectures built upon the foundational principles of Transformers promise a future where even more complex and nuanced NLP tasks can be effectively tackled. The potential for applications is vast, and the ongoing research within this area is dynamic and ever-evolving. This makes it an exciting field to follow and contribute to for aspiring AI researchers and developers alike. As the field progresses, we can expect even more sophisticated and efficient Transformer-based models that will continue to push the boundaries of what's possible in natural language understanding and generation.

Building a Simple Chatbot

Building even a simple chatbot requires a foundational understanding of NLP techniques. We've explored sophisticated architectures like Transformers, but the principles behind even a basic chatbot are surprisingly accessible. This project will demonstrate how to construct a rudimentary chatbot using Python and several key NLP libraries. The goal isn't to create a sophisticated, conversational AI, but rather to illustrate the core concepts and provide a stepping stone towards more complex projects.

Our chatbot will operate on a simple pattern-matching system. This means we'll pre-define a set of patterns – questions or phrases – and corresponding responses. When a user inputs text, the chatbot will compare it against these patterns. If a match (or a close enough match) is found, the corresponding response will be returned. This approach avoids the complexities of deep learning models, making it an ideal starting point for beginners.

First, we need to install the necessary libraries. We'll primarily use `NLTK` (Natural Language Toolkit) for text processing tasks like tokenization and stemming. `spaCy` provides advanced NLP features, but for this simple chatbot, NLTK's capabilities are sufficient. We'll also utilize the `random` library to introduce some variability in the chatbot's responses, preventing it from always giving the same answer. If you haven't already, install these libraries using pip:

```bash
pip install nltk spacy
python -m spacy download en_core_web_sm
```

```

The `spacy download en_core_web_sm` command downloads a small English language model. Larger models are available, offering improved accuracy, but they consume significantly more resources. For our simple chatbot, the small model is perfectly adequate.

Now, let's write the Python code. We'll start by defining our pattern-response pairs. We can store these in a dictionary where the keys are patterns (user input) and the values are the corresponding responses. Keep in mind that this is a simplified example. A real-world chatbot would require a much more extensive database of patterns and responses.

```python
import nltk
import random
from nltk.tokenize import word_tokenize
from nltk.stem import PorterStemmer

nltk.download('punkt')
nltk.download('stopwords')

patterns = {
"hello": ["Hi there!", "Hello!", "Hey!"],
"how are you": ["I'm doing well, thank you!", "I'm good, how about you?"],
"what's your name": ["I'm a simple chatbot.", "I don't have a name."],
"goodbye": ["Bye!", "See you later!", "Farewell!"],
"what is your purpose": ["I am here to assist you with simple queries.", "My purpose is to demonstrate basic chatbot functionality."],
"what can you do": ["I can answer simple questions based on predefined patterns.", "I can engage in basic

```python
    conversations."],
    "what time is it": ["I cannot tell time.", "Sorry, I don't have access to real-time information."],
    "tell me a joke": ["Why don't scientists trust atoms? Because they make up everything!", "Parallel lines have so much in common. It's a shame they'll never meet."],
    "default": ["I'm not sure I understand.", "Could you rephrase your question?"]
}

stemmer = PorterStemmer()
stop_words = set(nltk.corpus.stopwords.words('english'))

def preprocess_text(text):
    tokens = word_tokenize(text.lower())
    stemmed_tokens = [stemmer.stem(token) for token in tokens if token not in stop_words and token.isalnum()]
    return stemmed_tokens

def get_response(user_input):
    processed_input = preprocess_text(user_input)
    for pattern, responses in patterns.items():
        processed_pattern = preprocess_text(pattern)
        if all(word in processed_input for word in processed_pattern): return random.choice(responses)
    return random.choice(patterns["default"])

while True:
    user_input = input("You: ")
    if user_input.lower() == "quit":
        break
```

```
response = get_response(user input)
print("Chatbot:", response)
```
```
```

This code first preprocesses the user input by tokenizing it, removing stop words (common words like "the," "a," "is"), and stemming (reducing words to their root form). This simplifies the comparison process. The `get_response` function then iterates through the `patterns` dictionary, checking for matches. If a match is found, a random response from the corresponding list is returned; otherwise, a default response is provided. The `while` loop allows the chatbot to continue interacting with the user until the user types "quit."

This is a very basic example, and its limitations are apparent. It only understands very specific phrases and doesn't handle variations in sentence structure or complex queries. The accuracy is limited by the pattern matching; it doesn't understand the
meaning
of the text but merely matches keywords.

To improve this chatbot, we could incorporate more sophisticated NLP techniques. Instead of simple pattern matching, we could use techniques like:

Semantic Similarity:
Measuring the semantic similarity between the user input and the patterns using techniques like cosine similarity on word embeddings. Word embeddings, such as those generated by Word2Vec or GloVe, represent words as vectors in a high-dimensional space, where semantically similar words are closer together.

Intent Recognition:
Identifying the user's intent behind their input. This often involves using machine learning models trained on labeled datasets of user inputs and their corresponding intents.

Dialogue Management:
Managing the flow of the conversation, keeping track of the context, and remembering

previous interactions.

External Knowledge Bases:
Connecting the chatbot to external knowledge bases or APIs to allow it to access information beyond its predefined patterns.

Machine Learning Models:
Training machine learning models, such as sequence-to-sequence models or transformer networks, to generate more natural and contextually relevant responses.

Building a more advanced chatbot would require a substantial increase in complexity, involving training machine learning models on large datasets. However, this simple example provides a valuable starting point for understanding the fundamental principles of NLP and chatbot development. It demonstrates how even rudimentary NLP techniques can be used to create a functional, albeit limited, conversational agent. The journey from this basic chatbot to a sophisticated conversational AI involves a significant expansion of techniques and data, but this foundational example provides a solid framework to build upon. Further exploration of the libraries mentioned and investigation into more advanced NLP concepts will allow you to construct increasingly complex and intelligent chatbots. Remember to experiment, iterate, and constantly refine your approach as you delve deeper into the fascinating world of natural language processing.

Integrating Different AI Components

Integrating different AI components into a cohesive and functional AI assistant requires careful planning and execution. This process involves not just the technical integration of various AI modules, but also considerations of user experience, data management, and ethical implications. Let's delve into the specifics of building such an assistant, starting with the core components.

The foundation of our AI assistant will be Natural Language Processing (NLP). We've already explored NLP fundamentals in the previous chapter, covering text preprocessing, word embeddings, and the application of RNNs and Transformers. For our assistant, we'll leverage these techniques to enable the understanding and interpretation of user requests. This includes tasks like intent recognition – determining what the user wants to achieve – and entity extraction – identifying key pieces of information within the user's request, such as dates, locations, or names. For instance, if a user says, "Set a reminder for my dentist appointment tomorrow at 2 PM," the NLP module must identify the intent (setting a reminder), the entity "dentist appointment," the date ("tomorrow"), and the time ("2 PM").

Beyond basic intent and entity extraction, more sophisticated NLP techniques can enhance the assistant's capabilities. Sentiment analysis can help gauge the user's emotional state, allowing the assistant to respond appropriately. For example, a frustrated user might require a more empathetic response than a user making a simple request. Dialogue management is crucial for maintaining context across multiple turns of conversation. Without it, the assistant might fail to remember previous interactions, leading to frustrating experiences.

Consider a scenario where a user asks, "What's the weather like in London?" followed by "And in Paris?" The dialogue manager needs to maintain context and understand that the second query refers to weather, not a different topic entirely.

Speech recognition forms the input mechanism for our AI assistant. This component converts spoken language into text, allowing users to interact naturally using their voice. Various techniques, including Hidden Markov Models (HMMs) and Recurrent Neural Networks (RNNs), power modern speech recognition systems. The choice of technology depends on factors such as accuracy requirements, computational resources, and the specific characteristics of the user's voice. In addition to the accuracy of the transcription, the robustness of the speech recognition system against background noise and different accents is crucial. We must consider adding features to handle various speech patterns and accents to ensure a wider user base can effectively utilize the AI assistant.

The output mechanism, which converts the assistant's response from text back into speech, is just as important. Text-to-speech (TTS) systems, often based on concatenative synthesis or neural networks, are employed here. These systems transform the text generated by the NLP and other components into audible speech. The quality of the synthesized speech is paramount for user satisfaction; natural-sounding and easily understandable speech is essential for a positive user experience. We need to select TTS systems that provide high-quality, clear audio and that can adapt to different languages or even individual user preferences if possible.

Beyond NLP and speech recognition, many other AI components can enhance our AI assistant's capabilities. For example, integrating a knowledge base allows the assistant to access and retrieve relevant information to answer user queries. This knowledge base could be a structured database, a collection of documents, or even a combination of different data sources. Techniques like information retrieval, question answering, and knowledge graph traversal can help efficiently retrieve the required information. Consider a user asking, "What is the capital of France?" The knowledge base would contain this information, and the assistant would need the ability to retrieve and present it in a clear, understandable format.

Another valuable component is a task management system. This module allows the assistant to schedule appointments, set reminders, create to-do lists, and manage other user tasks. Integration with calendar applications or other productivity tools is often necessary for this functionality. Consider how the assistant might handle tasks that span multiple days or involve complex dependencies; the task management system needs to be robust enough to handle this complexity.

To ensure the AI assistant is user-friendly, the user interface (UI) design must be intuitive and engaging. A well-designed UI can significantly improve the overall user experience, even if the underlying AI capabilities are not perfect. The UI should present information clearly and concisely, guide users through interactions smoothly, and provide clear feedback on the assistant's actions. The choice of platform (mobile app, desktop application, web interface) will influence the UI design. Regardless of the chosen platform, usability testing should be part of the development process to identify and address any usability issues early on.

Furthermore, rigorous testing and refinement are critical for deploying a successful AI assistant. This involves testing different aspects of the system, including the accuracy of speech recognition, the reliability of the NLP engine, the correctness of the information retrieval system, and the responsiveness of the UI. Testing should involve diverse user groups to identify issues that might be overlooked otherwise.

Iterative refinement, based on user feedback and testing results, is essential for improving the performance and user experience of the AI assistant.

Finally, deploying and maintaining the AI assistant requires careful consideration. This includes choosing a suitable deployment platform (cloud, on-device), ensuring scalability to handle a growing user base, and establishing a system for monitoring performance and handling errors. Furthermore, ongoing development and enhancements are essential to keep the AI assistant up-to-date with advances in AI technology and to incorporate user feedback. Regular updates, bug fixes, and improvements in functionality are crucial for maintaining user engagement and satisfaction over the long term.

The successful integration of these AI components, combined with thoughtful UI design, thorough testing, and ongoing refinement, will result in a functional and helpful AI assistant. The process is iterative and requires a collaborative approach, involving expertise from various AI disciplines and a commitment to building a truly user-centric system. The journey from individual components to a complete AI assistant is a complex but rewarding undertaking, opening the door to a future of more intelligent and helpful AI companions.

Designing the User Interface

Designing a user-friendly interface is paramount to the success of any AI assistant. A poorly designed interface, no matter how sophisticated the underlying AI, will frustrate users and ultimately limit its adoption. Therefore, careful consideration must be given to several key aspects throughout the design process. This includes choosing the right input and output modalities, designing intuitive navigation, and incorporating effective feedback mechanisms. The goal is to create an interface that is not only aesthetically pleasing but also efficient, accessible, and enjoyable to use.

The first crucial decision is selecting appropriate input methods. While voice input offers a natural and intuitive interaction style, it is not without limitations. Background noise can interfere with accurate speech recognition, and some users might feel uncomfortable speaking to a machine, especially in public settings. Therefore, a multimodal approach, combining voice input with text-based input (e.g., typing or selecting options from a menu), often proves more robust and user-friendly. This allows users to select their preferred interaction method depending on the context and their comfort level. Consideration should also be given to supporting different input languages and accents, expanding the accessibility of your AI assistant to a broader audience. For example, the system could incorporate automatic language detection and translation capabilities.

Output modalities are equally important. The AI assistant should be able to respond in a clear, concise, and understandable manner. Text-based output is often preferred for complex or nuanced responses, allowing users to review the information at their own pace. However, visual aids such as images, charts, or maps can significantly enhance understanding, especially when dealing with spatial or visual information. Audio output, in the form of synthesized speech, is beneficial for hands-free operation or when users prefer to listen rather than read. Again, a multimodal approach, intelligently combining text, audio, and visuals, often creates the most engaging and informative user experience. The system must adapt its output style based on the user's preferences and the nature of the query.

Designing intuitive navigation is crucial for usability. The user interface should guide users smoothly through the interaction process, making it easy to find the information or functionality they need. A clear and hierarchical structure, with well-defined menus and buttons, is essential. Avoid overwhelming users with excessive options or complex workflows. Consider employing visual cues, such as icons and color-coding, to enhance navigation and improve information comprehension. The system should also incorporate robust search functionality, allowing users to quickly find specific information or commands. Employing techniques such as autocomplete and predictive text significantly reduces the effort required by users, improving efficiency and overall satisfaction.

Effective feedback is essential for a positive user experience. The AI assistant should provide clear and timely feedback to the user's actions, letting them know that their input has been received and processed. This could involve simple visual cues, such as loading indicators or confirmation messages, or more sophisticated feedback mechanisms, such as progress bars or detailed explanations of the AI's reasoning process. In cases of errors or unexpected situations, the assistant should provide informative and helpful error messages, guiding the user towards a resolution. Avoid using technical jargon or cryptic error codes; instead, provide plain-language explanations that are easily understandable. The system must gracefully handle unexpected inputs or situations, preventing abrupt crashes or confusing error messages.

Personalization is another key aspect of a user-friendly interface. The system should adapt to the user's individual needs and preferences over time. This could involve learning the user's communication style, preferred input methods, and frequently accessed functions. Personalized recommendations and suggestions can also enhance the user experience, offering relevant information or services based on the user's past behavior and preferences. However, it's crucial to balance personalization with privacy concerns, ensuring that user data is collected and used responsibly. Transparency is key: users should be aware of how their data is being used and have control over their privacy settings.

Accessibility is a critical consideration that often gets overlooked. The AI assistant should be accessible to users with disabilities, including those with visual, auditory, motor, or cognitive impairments. This means adhering to accessibility guidelines, such as WCAG (Web Content Accessibility Guidelines), and incorporating features such as screen reader compatibility, keyboard navigation, and adjustable font sizes. Support for assistive technologies is essential to ensure inclusivity and equal access to the AI assistant's capabilities.

The design process should be iterative, involving user testing and feedback at each stage. Usability testing can identify potential usability issues early on, allowing for timely adjustments and improvements. Gather feedback from a diverse group of users, representing different demographics, technical skills, and accessibility needs. Analyze user feedback carefully and use it to refine the design, ensuring that the interface meets the needs and expectations of its target audience. User testing should not be a one-time event but an ongoing process throughout the development lifecycle.

Beyond functionality, the visual design of the interface plays a significant role in user experience. A visually appealing and consistent design enhances user engagement and trust. Use a clear and consistent visual language, with appropriate typography, color palettes, and imagery. The interface should be uncluttered and easy on the eyes, avoiding excessive animations or distracting elements. Consider employing design principles such as Gestalt principles to enhance visual organization and comprehension. A well-designed interface fosters a positive emotional connection with the user,
making the interaction more enjoyable and less stressful.

Finally, consider the platform on which the AI assistant will be deployed. The interface should be optimized for the target platform, whether it's a desktop computer, a mobile device, or a smart speaker. Different platforms have different user interface conventions and constraints, so the design must adapt accordingly. Ensure that the interface is responsive and adapts gracefully to different screen sizes and orientations. Optimizing for performance is also crucial, ensuring that the interface is fast, reliable, and responsive, even under heavy load.

The design of the user interface is a complex and multifaceted process, requiring careful planning, iterative development, and ongoing refinement. By considering the factors discussed above—input and output modalities, intuitive navigation, effective feedback, personalization, accessibility, iterative design, visual design, and platform considerations—we can create an AI assistant interface that is not only functional but also user-friendly, engaging, and enjoyable to use. The ultimate goal is to create an AI assistant that seamlessly integrates into users' lives, offering helpful assistance in a natural and intuitive way. A well-designed interface is the key to unlocking the full potential of the underlying AI, transforming it from a sophisticated piece of technology into a truly helpful and valued companion.

Developing Core Functionality

Now that we've meticulously crafted a user-friendly interface for our AI assistant, it's time to delve into the heart of the matter: implementing its core functionality. This involves bringing to life the features that will actually make our assistant useful and engaging for the user. We'll focus on three crucial areas: task management, information retrieval, and communication. Each of these requires a different approach, drawing on various AI techniques we've explored throughout this book.

Let's begin with
task management
. The ability to manage tasks efficiently is a hallmark of a productive AI assistant.
This goes beyond simple reminders; we're aiming for intelligent task scheduling, prioritization, and dependency tracking. This requires a sophisticated understanding of natural language, enabling the assistant to parse user requests like, "Remind me to buy milk tomorrow morning after I pick up the dry cleaning," and correctly interpret the dependencies (picking up dry cleaning must happen before buying milk).

To achieve this, we need to employ several techniques. First, we'll leverage natural language processing (NLP) to understand the user's instructions. This involves tokenization, part-of-speech tagging, named entity recognition (to identify "milk," "dry cleaning," and "tomorrow morning"), and dependency parsing to understand the relationships between different parts of the sentence. We'll use libraries like spaCy and NLTK for these tasks, building upon our previous exploration of NLP in earlier chapters.

Furthermore, we need a robust task representation. We might use a structured data format, such as JSON, to represent each task, including its description, due date, priority, and any dependencies on other tasks. A database, such as SQLite or PostgreSQL, will be used to store and manage this task data persistently. The assistant will then use algorithms to schedule tasks optimally, perhaps employing priority queues or graph algorithms to handle dependencies. For example, if a task depends on the completion of another, the scheduling algorithm will ensure the dependent task isn't scheduled until its prerequisite is fulfilled.

The next core functionality is **information retrieval**. Our AI assistant needs to be able to answer questions accurately and efficiently. This requires access to a vast knowledge base and powerful search capabilities. A simple keyword search won't suffice; we'll need to incorporate more sophisticated techniques.

One approach is to utilize a vector database. This involves representing both questions and answers as vectors in a high-dimensional space. The similarity between vectors can then be used to retrieve the most relevant answers to a given question. This allows for semantic search, enabling the assistant to understand the meaning of the question, even if it doesn't contain exact keywords present in the answer. Libraries like FAISS (Facebook AI Similarity Search) or Annoy (Spotify's Approximate Nearest Neighbors) are well-suited for this purpose.

We can also incorporate knowledge graphs. A knowledge graph represents information as a network of interconnected entities and their relationships. This allows the assistant to reason about information and answer complex questions that require understanding relationships between different concepts. For instance, if a user asks, "What is the capital of the country where the Amazon rainforest is located?", the assistant can traverse the knowledge graph to find the answer (Brazil, Brasilia). Tools like Neo4j provide powerful capabilities for building and querying knowledge graphs.

Finally, and perhaps most importantly, is **communication**.

This encompasses how the AI assistant interacts with the user—the natural language generation (NLG) component. Simply providing factual answers isn't enough; the assistant needs to communicate information clearly, concisely, and in a natural, conversational style.

This requires more advanced NLP techniques, including text generation models. We can leverage transformer-based models, like those found in the Hugging Face Transformers library, which have proven highly effective in generating human-quality text. These models are trained on massive datasets of text and code, allowing them to learn the nuances of natural language and produce coherent, contextually relevant responses. Fine-tuning these models on a specific dataset related to the assistant's domain will significantly improve their performance.

However, merely generating grammatically correct sentences isn't enough; the assistant needs to maintain a consistent conversational style, personalize responses, and handle different user intents effectively. This necessitates designing a dialogue management system. Such a system tracks the conversation's context, manages the flow of dialogue, and selects appropriate responses based on the user's input and the conversation history.

To ensure a smooth and natural interaction, we should consider incorporating features like:

Contextual awareness:
The assistant should remember previous interactions within the conversation and use that information to inform its responses.

Personality:
We can inject personality into the assistant's responses by tailoring the tone and style of the language used.

Error handling:
The assistant should gracefully handle situations where it doesn't understand the user's request or encounters errors. Instead of abruptly failing, it should provide helpful feedback and possibly request clarification. **Proactive assistance:**
The assistant could anticipate user needs and offer relevant suggestions or information proactively. For example, if it notices the user is frequently scheduling meetings, it could suggest optimizing their calendar.

Integrating these three core functionalities – task management, information retrieval, and communication – requires careful planning and coordination. We'll need to design well-defined interfaces between the different components, ensuring data flows smoothly and consistently.
This might involve using message queues or other asynchronous communication mechanisms to handle concurrent requests and avoid performance bottlenecks.

Testing and iterative refinement are crucial throughout the development process. We should thoroughly test each component individually and then test the entire system as a whole to identify and resolve any integration issues. User feedback is essential for identifying areas for improvement and ensuring the AI assistant meets user needs and expectations.

This detailed implementation of the core functionality lays the foundation for a truly intelligent and helpful AI assistant. By combining advanced AI techniques with careful design and thorough testing, we can create an assistant that seamlessly integrates into users' lives, providing valuable assistance and enhancing their productivity. The journey from concept to a fully functional AI assistant is challenging but incredibly rewarding, showcasing the power and potential of artificial intelligence. The next chapter will delve into the deployment and scalability considerations for our AI assistant, ensuring it can handle a growing user base and adapt to evolving needs.

Testing and Refinement

The successful deployment of our AI assistant hinges not just on its initial functionality but also on its robustness and adaptability. Thorough testing and iterative refinement are crucial steps in ensuring its performance and user satisfaction. This process involves a multi-pronged approach, encompassing unit testing, integration testing, user acceptance testing, and ongoing monitoring and improvement.

Unit testing focuses on individual components of the AI assistant. For instance, we would test the natural language processing (NLP) module separately to ensure accurate parsing of user inputs and appropriate responses. This might involve feeding the NLP module a wide range of sentences, including grammatically correct and incorrect ones, ambiguous phrases, and sentences containing slang or colloquialisms. We would evaluate the accuracy of its intent recognition, entity extraction, and sentiment analysis capabilities. For each test case, we define expected outputs and compare them to the actual outputs, meticulously documenting any discrepancies. Unit tests help identify and resolve bugs early in the development lifecycle, preventing them from propagating to the higher levels of integration. The use of a robust testing framework, such as pytest in Python, is crucial for efficient and repeatable unit testing. Detailed logging of test results facilitates easy identification of problematic areas.

Integration testing involves testing the interactions between different modules of the AI assistant. This is where we verify whether the NLP module seamlessly integrates with the task management module, the information retrieval module, and the speech synthesis module. For example, we would test a scenario where a user requests information, which requires the NLP module to correctly understand the request, the information retrieval module to find the relevant data, and the speech synthesis module to deliver the information clearly and concisely. Integration tests are essential for discovering inconsistencies and communication bottlenecks between different modules. We need to ensure that data transfer between modules is efficient and error-free. We should consider various failure scenarios, such as network outages or database errors, and implement appropriate error handling mechanisms. This rigorous testing phase can involve the creation of simulated user interactions or utilizing a sandboxed environment that mirrors the real-world deployment conditions.

User acceptance testing (UAT) is a critical phase that involves real users interacting with the AI assistant. This testing allows us to gather feedback on the user experience, identify usability issues, and gauge the overall effectiveness of the assistant. We should recruit a diverse group of users with varying levels of technological proficiency to obtain a representative sample of feedback. UAT might involve having users complete a series of predefined tasks using the assistant, providing feedback through surveys, interviews, or observation sessions. We need to pay close attention to user comments and suggestions regarding the system's performance, accuracy, and intuitive ease of use. UAT provides invaluable insights into areas needing improvement from a user's perspective. The data collected during UAT should be analyzed to identify potential issues and inform further development iterations.

Beyond the initial testing phases, continuous monitoring and refinement are essential. Once deployed, the AI assistant will need to be continually monitored for performance and to adapt to evolving user needs and data patterns. This monitoring phase might involve setting up alerts for error conditions, tracking key performance indicators (KPIs) such as response times and task completion rates, and analyzing user feedback through analytics tools. This continuous feedback loop is vital in ensuring the long-term success of the AI assistant. The monitoring process should also include analyzing the data generated by the AI assistant's usage to identify patterns and trends that can inform future improvements. For example, we could analyze the types of requests most frequently made, the frequency of errors, and the areas where users struggle to achieve their goals using the assistant. This data-driven approach helps make informed decisions about feature enhancements, performance optimization, and bug fixes.

Furthermore, the AI assistant's performance can be optimized through techniques such as hyperparameter tuning and model retraining. Hyperparameter tuning involves systematically adjusting the parameters of the AI models used within the assistant to improve its accuracy and efficiency. This often involves experimenting with different parameter settings and evaluating the impact on the assistant's performance using metrics such as precision, recall, and F1-score. Model retraining is another critical process where the AI models are updated with new data to enhance their performance over time. This process is particularly relevant when the data used to train the initial model becomes outdated or when new data reveals previously unseen patterns. Retraining can significantly improve the accuracy and effectiveness of the AI assistant, enabling it to adapt to changing user needs and environmental conditions. Regular retraining schedules, coupled with meticulous data cleaning and preprocessing, are essential for maintaining the assistant's long-term performance. We should establish a robust data pipeline that facilitates regular data collection, preprocessing, and feeding into the retraining process.

Finally, rigorous testing is a critical part of ensuring the ethical considerations are addressed. We must vigilantly monitor for any indication of bias in the assistant's responses, ensuring that it doesn't perpetuate or amplify societal prejudices. This might involve regularly auditing the data used to train the assistant, testing the assistant's responses with different demographics and cultural backgrounds, and employing methods to identify and mitigate potential biases. The ongoing assessment of ethical considerations is not a one-time process, but rather an ongoing commitment throughout the assistant's lifespan. This iterative testing, refinement, and monitoring process is an integral part of the development cycle and should be considered a continuous and evolving aspect of building a robust and ethical AI assistant. The commitment to comprehensive testing is not merely a technical exercise but also a fundamental aspect of responsible AI development. By carefully considering the strategies detailed here, we pave the way for creating an AI assistant that is not only functional but also trustworthy, reliable, and ethically sound.

Deployment and Future Enhancements

Deployment of our AI assistant requires a multifaceted strategy that extends beyond simply making the software available. We need to consider the infrastructure required to support its operation, the user interface, and the mechanisms for ongoing maintenance and improvement. The choice of deployment platform is critical. Will it be a cloud-based solution, offering scalability and accessibility, or a locally hosted system, prioritizing data security and control? Cloud platforms like AWS, Google Cloud, or Azure provide robust infrastructure and managed services, simplifying deployment and maintenance. However, this comes with potential concerns about data privacy and vendor lock-in. A locally hosted solution, on the other hand, offers greater control but necessitates managing the underlying infrastructure, including server hardware, networking, and security. This approach is often more complex and resource-intensive.

Regardless of the chosen platform, a well-defined deployment pipeline is essential. This pipeline should automate the process of building, testing, and deploying the assistant, minimizing manual intervention and ensuring consistency. Continuous integration and continuous deployment (CI/CD) practices are highly recommended. These involve automating the integration of code changes from multiple developers, running automated tests, and deploying the updated assistant to the target environment. Tools like Jenkins, GitLab CI, or GitHub Actions can significantly streamline this process. Version control is paramount, allowing for easy rollback to previous versions in case of unforeseen issues. A robust logging and monitoring system is critical for tracking the assistant's performance, identifying potential problems, and providing insights for future improvements. Metrics such as response time, error rates, and user engagement should be meticulously tracked and analyzed.

The user interface (UI) plays a crucial role in user experience. A well-designed UI ensures that users can interact with the assistant intuitively and effectively. Considerations include the choice of input methods (voice, text, or a combination), the presentation of the assistant's responses, and the overall aesthetic appeal of the interface. The UI should be accessible to users with diverse abilities, adhering to accessibility guidelines such as WCAG (Web Content Accessibility Guidelines). User feedback mechanisms, such as integrated surveys or feedback forms, are essential for gathering information about user experiences and identifying areas for improvement. Regular updates to the UI based on user feedback can significantly enhance user satisfaction and adoption.

Security is a paramount concern in the deployment of any AI system, particularly one that handles sensitive user data. Robust security measures must be implemented to protect the assistant from unauthorized access, data breaches, and malicious attacks. These measures might include secure authentication and authorization mechanisms, data encryption both in transit and at rest, regular security audits, and vulnerability scanning. The selection of secure libraries and frameworks is crucial during the development process. Furthermore, a comprehensive security plan should be in place, outlining procedures for responding to security incidents and ensuring business continuity. Regular security training for the development and operations teams is also necessary to maintain a high level of security awareness.

Beyond the initial deployment, ongoing maintenance and updates are essential for the long-term success of the AI assistant. This involves regular monitoring of performance, addressing bugs, and incorporating new features and functionalities based on user feedback and evolving needs. A robust feedback loop should be established to collect user input, allowing for iterative improvement of the assistant's capabilities. This necessitates a clear process for managing updates, including testing, deploying, and monitoring the impact of changes. The system should be designed for scalability, allowing it to handle increasing user loads and data volumes without significant performance degradation. Planning for future scalability is crucial, potentially involving transitioning to more powerful hardware or optimizing algorithms for efficiency.

Future enhancements to the AI assistant should be guided by a roadmap that outlines specific goals and timelines. This roadmap should incorporate user feedback, emerging technologies, and anticipated future trends. For example, incorporating more sophisticated natural language processing techniques could improve the assistant's ability to understand complex queries and provide more nuanced responses. Integrating with other services and platforms, such as calendar applications, email clients, or social media platforms, could expand the assistant's functionality and provide users with a more seamless and integrated experience. The addition of multimodal capabilities, allowing the assistant to process and respond to various input modalities (text, images, audio), would also enhance its versatility and user engagement.

Machine learning model retraining is a critical aspect of ongoing improvement. As the assistant interacts with users and accumulates more data, its performance can be enhanced through periodic retraining of its underlying models. This retraining should be done using a well-defined process, including data cleaning, feature engineering, model selection, and evaluation. The retraining process should be automated as much as possible, using CI/CD pipelines to streamline the deployment of updated models. It's essential to monitor the performance of the retrained models, ensuring that they continue to meet the desired accuracy and efficiency standards. This continuous learning aspect is crucial for maintaining the assistant's relevance and effectiveness over time.

Ethical considerations must remain central to future developments. Ongoing monitoring for bias in the assistant's responses is critical. This necessitates employing techniques to identify and mitigate biases present in the training data and algorithms. Regular audits of the data used to train the assistant are necessary to ensure fairness and prevent the perpetuation of harmful stereotypes. Transparency in the assistant's decision-making processes is also crucial. Users should have a clear understanding of how the assistant arrives at its responses, fostering trust and accountability. This requires careful consideration of explainable AI (XAI) techniques, aiming to make the assistant's reasoning processes more understandable and interpretable.

The long-term vision for the AI assistant might involve creating a personalized and adaptive experience for each user. This involves leveraging techniques like user profiling, preference modeling, and reinforcement learning to tailor the assistant's responses and functionalities to individual user needs and preferences. This level of personalization requires careful consideration of user privacy and data security. The use of federated learning techniques, which allow for model training on decentralized data without compromising user privacy, could be explored. Ultimately, the goal should be to create an AI assistant that is not only technically proficient but also ethically sound, respectful of user privacy, and continuously improving based on user feedback and advancements in the field of AI.

The development of the AI assistant is an ongoing journey, requiring continuous innovation, adaptation, and a commitment to ethical principles. The deployment process and future enhancements should be viewed as integral parts of a larger iterative process, emphasizing robust testing, user feedback, and responsible AI development. By incorporating these considerations, we can create an AI assistant that is not just a tool, but a valuable and trustworthy partner for users. This commitment to responsible AI development is crucial not only for the success of the project, but also for its positive impact on society. The ongoing process of improvement should always be guided by ethical considerations and a focus on user wellbeing. The future of AI assistants lies in their ability to seamlessly integrate into our lives, providing genuine value while respecting our privacy and upholding our societal values. This requires continued research, innovation, and a commitment to developing AI systems that are both powerful and responsible.

Bias in AI Systems

Bias, a pervasive issue in many aspects of human society, unfortunately finds its way into the artificial intelligence systems we create. This is not a malicious intent, but rather a consequence of the data used to train these systems and the inherent biases present within that data. AI algorithms, powerful as they are, are ultimately only as good as the data they are trained on. If that data reflects existing societal biases, the AI system will inevitably learn and perpetuate those biases, leading to unfair or discriminatory outcomes.

One primary source of bias stems from the datasets used for training. These datasets are often compiled from real-world sources, which inherently contain biases reflecting the prejudices and inequalities present in our society. For instance, a facial recognition system trained predominantly on images of light-skinned individuals may perform poorly when identifying individuals with darker skin tones. This isn't because the algorithm is inherently racist, but because it has learned to recognize faces based on the limited and biased data it was exposed to. Similarly, a loan application algorithm trained on historical data that reflects discriminatory lending practices may unfairly deny loans to certain demographic groups, even if those groups are now equally creditworthy.

The problem is further exacerbated by the way data is collected and labeled. Data collection methods can inadvertently introduce bias. Consider a dataset used to train a system for identifying job applicants. If the data predominantly includes applications from a specific demographic group, the AI may learn to favor candidates from that group, leading to systematic discrimination against others. Similarly, the way data is labeled can introduce bias. If the labels used in training reflect subjective human judgments, they may incorporate personal biases which the AI will then learn and reproduce. For example, if human annotators systematically mislabel images of women in certain professions, the AI will subsequently reinforce that bias in its predictions.

Another critical aspect is the algorithmic bias itself. Even with unbiased data, the design and implementation of the algorithm can still introduce bias. The choice of algorithm, the selection of features, and the hyperparameters used in training all impact the final outcome. A poorly designed algorithm may unintentionally amplify existing biases present in the data or introduce new ones. For instance, a simpler algorithm might rely on easily available but potentially biased features, while a more complex model might be able to identify and correct for these biases, requiring a far greater amount of high-quality data and significant expertise in avoiding unintended bias. The choice of algorithm therefore becomes crucial, and the selection must be carefully considered in light of potential bias.

The impact of bias in AI systems is far-reaching and can have severe consequences. Biased AI systems can lead to unfair or discriminatory outcomes in various areas, including hiring, loan applications, criminal justice, and healthcare. In hiring, a biased system may systematically exclude qualified candidates from certain demographic groups. In loan applications, a biased system may unfairly deny loans to creditworthy individuals based on their race or gender. In the criminal justice system, a biased system might unfairly target individuals from specific communities. In healthcare, a biased system may misdiagnose or provide inadequate care to certain patient populations. These are not hypothetical situations; they are real-world problems arising from biased

AI systems, showcasing the significant societal harm that can result.

Mitigating bias in AI systems requires a multi-faceted approach that addresses the entire AI development lifecycle. Firstly, it's crucial to ensure that the data used for training is representative and unbiased. This involves careful data collection, cleaning, and preprocessing to identify and remove or mitigate existing biases. Techniques like data augmentation, which involves artificially increasing the diversity of the data, can help address imbalances in datasets. Careful consideration must be given to source data, considering factors like sampling methods and the possible influence of human bias during data collection. Using diverse datasets that adequately represent various demographics is paramount.

Secondly, it's essential to carefully evaluate AI models for bias throughout the development process. This requires the use of appropriate metrics that go beyond simple accuracy measures and can explicitly identify and quantify bias. There are a range of fairness metrics that can be used to assess the fairness of a model's predictions across different demographic groups. For example, examining the disparities in outcomes for different protected groups (gender, race, ethnicity, etc.) can highlight potential biases. Regular monitoring and auditing of deployed systems are crucial to detecting and addressing any emerging biases.

Thirdly, algorithmic fairness should be integrated into the design of AI systems from the outset. This involves considering ethical implications and fairness constraints during algorithm design and implementation. Incorporating fairness-aware algorithms, which explicitly aim to mitigate bias, can improve the fairness of AI systems. This requires a strong collaboration between AI developers, ethicists, and domain experts to ensure that fairness is a central consideration throughout the development process. Moreover, transparency and explainability in AI models are increasingly vital to understand how decisions are made and identify potential sources of bias.

Beyond technical solutions, promoting diversity and inclusion within the AI development community is crucial. A diverse team of developers, researchers, and stakeholders can bring different perspectives and experiences to the development process, leading to a more inclusive and equitable outcome. This approach aims to reduce unconscious biases and ensure that diverse viewpoints are incorporated throughout the project's lifecycle.

Furthermore, the legal and regulatory landscape around AI is evolving, with increased focus on addressing bias and promoting fairness. Regulations and guidelines are being developed to ensure accountability and transparency in the use of AI systems, particularly in high-stakes decision-making processes. Understanding and complying with these regulations is essential for responsible AI development and deployment. This includes adhering to guidelines and best practices that emphasize the ethical development and use of AI, and actively promoting transparent and responsible AI practices.

In conclusion, bias in AI systems is a significant challenge that requires a concerted effort from the entire AI community to address. By employing a multi-faceted approach that includes careful data curation, bias detection and mitigation techniques, ethical algorithm design, and a commitment to diversity and inclusion, we can build AI systems that are fair, equitable, and beneficial to all members of society. The responsibility for mitigating bias rests with everyone involved in the development, deployment, and use of AI, and continued research and dialogue are critical to address this complex issue effectively. Only through collective action and ongoing vigilance can we harness the power of AI while mitigating its potential for harm.

Privacy Concerns in AI

The pervasiveness of data in AI systems necessitates a thorough examination of privacy concerns. AI's ability to learn and improve relies heavily on vast datasets, often encompassing sensitive personal information. This reliance raises critical questions about the ethical implications of data collection, storage, and usage, demanding careful consideration of individual rights and societal well-being. The very nature of AI, its ability to identify patterns and make predictions, inherently increases the risk of unauthorized access to sensitive personal information and the potential for misuse.

One of the most significant privacy challenges is the sheer volume of data collected. Modern AI systems, particularly those employing deep learning techniques, require massive datasets for effective training. This often leads to the collection of data far beyond what is strictly necessary for the intended purpose. For instance, a facial recognition system might collect images not only of individuals' faces but also of their surroundings, potentially capturing sensitive details about their lives and locations. Similarly, an AI-powered health application might collect detailed medical history and lifestyle information, raising concerns about the security and potential misuse of this sensitive data. The sheer scale of data collection increases the potential attack surface, making data breaches more likely and more damaging.

The issue extends beyond the quantity of data to its sensitivity. Many AI applications rely on personal data that is considered highly sensitive under privacy regulations like GDPR (General Data Protection Regulation) or CCPA (California Consumer Privacy Act). This includes information such as financial data, health records, location data, biometric information (fingerprints, facial scans), genetic information, and even seemingly innocuous data like browsing history and social media activity, which, when aggregated and analyzed, can reveal intimate details about an individual's life, preferences, and relationships. The potential for these data points to be linked together, creating a detailed profile, further enhances the privacy risk.

Furthermore, the opacity of many AI algorithms presents a significant challenge. The complex nature of deep learning models often makes it difficult to understand how they arrive at their conclusions. This "black box" nature hinders accountability and makes it difficult to assess whether the AI system is respecting individual privacy rights. If a system makes a decision that negatively impacts an individual, it can be nearly impossible to determine why, let alone identify and correct any privacy violations. This lack of transparency undermines trust and makes it challenging to ensure compliance with data protection regulations.

Data breaches are another significant concern. The increasing reliance on cloud-based storage for AI data makes systems vulnerable to cyberattacks and data breaches. A single breach can expose the personal information of millions of individuals, leading to identity theft, financial loss, and reputational damage. The scale of such breaches, particularly given the often-sensitive nature of the data involved, can have far-reaching consequences for individuals and society.

The use of AI for surveillance is another significant area of privacy concern. Facial recognition technology, for example, is increasingly deployed in public spaces, raising concerns about mass surveillance and the potential for abuse. The lack of transparency and accountability in many surveillance applications exacerbates these concerns. Similarly, the use of AI to analyze social media data to predict individual behavior raises concerns about potential censorship and manipulation.

The ethical challenges are further compounded by the lack of clear and consistent regulatory frameworks for AI systems. Current data protection laws, while important, are often not designed to adequately address the unique challenges posed by AI. The rapidly evolving nature of AI technology makes it difficult for lawmakers to keep pace, creating a regulatory gap that allows potentially harmful practices to flourish. This lack of clear guidelines leaves individuals vulnerable and creates uncertainty for developers and organizations deploying AI systems.

Addressing these privacy challenges requires a multi-pronged approach. Firstly, stronger data protection regulations are crucial. These regulations should be designed specifically to address the unique challenges posed by AI, including the use of sensitive data, the opacity of algorithms, and the potential for mass surveillance. These regulations should ensure transparency and accountability, enabling individuals to understand how their data is being used and to exercise their rights.

Secondly, the development of privacy-preserving AI techniques is vital. These techniques, such as federated learning and differential privacy, enable the development and deployment of AI systems without requiring the direct access to sensitive data. Federated learning allows training on decentralized data sources without directly transferring data, while differential privacy adds noise to individual data points to protect their identities while preserving aggregate patterns. These are essential steps in mitigating privacy risks inherent in large-scale AI deployments.

Thirdly, increased transparency and explainability in AI systems are crucial. The development of techniques to make AI algorithms more interpretable is paramount. This allows developers to understand how their systems are making decisions, identify potential privacy violations, and ensure compliance with regulations. This transparency also fosters trust and allows individuals to hold developers accountable for any misuse of their data.

Finally, fostering a culture of ethical AI development and deployment is essential. This requires educating developers and organizations about the ethical implications of AI and providing them with the tools and resources they need to develop and deploy AI systems responsibly. Ethical guidelines and codes of conduct can provide a framework for ethical decision-making, and promoting collaboration between researchers, policymakers, and industry stakeholders is critical to ensure the responsible development and deployment of AI. The active involvement of individuals in the conversations surrounding AI ethics is equally important. They should have a voice in shaping policies that govern how their data is used.

In conclusion, the privacy concerns related to AI are substantial and multifaceted. Addressing these challenges requires a concerted effort from researchers, policymakers, industry, and the public. By combining robust regulations, innovative privacy-preserving techniques, enhanced transparency, and a strong commitment to ethical AI development, we can harness the transformative power of AI while safeguarding individual privacy and upholding fundamental human rights. Only through a multi-faceted approach that prioritizes ethics and accountability can we ensure that AI benefits society without compromising the privacy of its citizens. The future of AI depends on our ability to address these fundamental challenges effectively. Failure to do so risks not only undermining trust in AI but also creating a society where technology is used to undermine basic rights. The pursuit of responsible AI is therefore not merely an ethical imperative; it is essential for the long-term health and well-being of both individuals and society as a whole.

Responsible AI Development

Building responsible AI systems requires a multifaceted approach that goes beyond simply creating functional algorithms. It demands a deep commitment to ethical considerations throughout the entire development lifecycle, from initial design to deployment and ongoing monitoring. This commitment must encompass fairness, transparency, accountability, and privacy. Ignoring these principles can lead to AI systems that perpetuate biases, infringe on individual rights, or even cause harm.

One of the fundamental pillars of responsible AI development is fairness. AI systems are trained on data, and if that data reflects existing societal biases, the resulting system will likely perpetuate and even amplify those biases. For instance, a facial recognition system trained primarily on images of individuals with lighter skin tones may perform poorly when identifying individuals with darker skin tones, leading to potential misidentification and unfair consequences in law enforcement or security applications. To mitigate this, careful attention must be paid to data curation. This includes actively seeking diverse and representative datasets, employing techniques to detect and mitigate biases within the data, and rigorously evaluating the fairness of the resulting AI system across different demographic groups. Furthermore, ongoing monitoring and auditing of the system's performance are crucial to identify and address emerging biases over time, as new data is ingested and the system adapts. Techniques like fairness-aware machine learning algorithms are also being developed to explicitly incorporate fairness constraints into the training process.

Transparency is another critical aspect. Understanding how an AI system arrives at its decisions is crucial for building trust and ensuring accountability. "Black box" AI systems, where the decision-making process is opaque, make it difficult to identify and rectify errors, biases, or unintended consequences. Promoting transparency involves developing techniques to explain the system's reasoning, such as creating explainable AI (XAI) models that provide insights into the factors contributing to a particular decision. This might involve visualizing the internal workings of the model, identifying the most influential features, or generating human-readable explanations. Moreover, documentation of the entire development process, including data sources, model architecture, training procedures, and evaluation metrics, is essential for transparency and allows for easier auditing and replication. This transparency also empowers users to understand how the AI system affects them and to challenge decisions if necessary.

Accountability is inextricably linked to transparency. When an AI system makes a mistake or causes harm, it is crucial to be able to determine who is responsible. This requires establishing clear lines of responsibility throughout the development and deployment lifecycle. This involves defining roles and responsibilities for different stakeholders, including data scientists, engineers, managers, and even legal and ethical advisors. Mechanisms for reporting and investigating incidents involving AI systems should also be in place. Furthermore, legal frameworks and regulations are essential to ensure that those responsible for developing and deploying AI systems are held accountable for their actions. This may involve establishing liability frameworks for AI-related harms and designing regulatory mechanisms to oversee the development and use of AI in critical applications. The development of standardized auditing procedures is crucial to ensure consistent evaluation of AI systems' ethical performance and accountability.

Privacy is a fundamental human right, and AI systems must be developed and deployed in a way that respects this right. AI systems often rely on vast amounts of data, much of which may be sensitive personal information. Protecting this information is paramount. This necessitates the implementation of robust data security measures to prevent unauthorized access, use, or disclosure of personal data. Privacy-preserving techniques, such as differential privacy and federated learning, allow AI systems to be trained on sensitive data without directly accessing or storing it. Moreover, transparency regarding data collection and usage practices is essential, so users understand how their data is being used and can provide informed consent. Compliance with relevant data privacy regulations, such as GDPR and CCPA, is also crucial for ensuring responsible handling of personal data. Furthermore, data minimization techniques should be employed, ensuring that only the necessary data is collected and used for AI system development.

Beyond these core principles, responsible AI development requires a broader cultural shift within the AI community. This includes promoting ethical education and training for AI developers, fostering a culture of responsible innovation, and engaging with broader societal stakeholders in discussions about the ethical implications of AI. Open collaboration and knowledge sharing within the AI community are essential to identify and address emerging ethical challenges. Active participation in the development of ethical guidelines and standards for AI is crucial, and researchers, developers, and policymakers must work together to create a framework that promotes the responsible development and use of AI. Furthermore, promoting diversity and inclusion within the AI community is essential to ensure that AI systems are developed and deployed in a way that reflects the diverse needs and perspectives of all stakeholders.

The integration of ethical considerations into the software development lifecycle (SDLC) for AI is crucial. This means incorporating ethical reviews and assessments at various stages of development. Ethical impact assessments should be conducted to anticipate potential risks and harms associated with an AI system. These assessments should consider a range of factors, including potential biases, privacy implications, and the potential for misuse. Furthermore, continuous monitoring and evaluation of the system's performance, in terms of both effectiveness and ethical implications, are essential to identify and address any emerging problems. Regular ethical audits should be undertaken to review the system's performance against predetermined ethical standards. This iterative process helps to ensure that the AI system remains aligned with ethical principles throughout its lifecycle.

Responsible AI development also necessitates a focus on user experience and accessibility. AI systems should be designed to be user-friendly, inclusive, and accessible to people of all abilities and backgrounds. This requires careful consideration of user interface design, accessibility features, and the potential impact on marginalized groups. For instance, AI systems should be designed to be usable by individuals with disabilities, ensuring that they can interact with the system effectively and independently. Moreover, systems should be designed to be understandable and interpretable, allowing users to comprehend how the system arrives at its decisions and to challenge those decisions if needed.

Ultimately, responsible AI development is not merely a set of technical guidelines; it's a fundamental shift in how we approach the design, development, and deployment of AI systems. It requires a commitment to ethical principles, a focus on transparency and accountability, and a deep understanding of the societal impact of AI. By prioritizing these principles, we can harness the immense potential of AI while mitigating its risks and ensuring that it serves humanity's best interests. The challenge lies not just in building powerful AI systems, but in building AI systems that are just, fair, and beneficial for all. The future of AI hinges on our ability to meet this challenge. Continuous learning, adaptation, and a commitment to ethical reflection are crucial for responsible AI development, ensuring that this transformative technology benefits society as a whole. Failure to prioritize ethics and responsibility risks undermining trust in AI and creating a world where technology exacerbates existing inequalities and injustices. The ongoing dialogue and collaboration between researchers, developers, policymakers, and the public are essential to navigate this complex landscape effectively.

The Social Impact of AI

The pervasive influence of AI extends far beyond the technical realm, deeply impacting various facets of society. Understanding these societal implications is crucial for responsible AI development and deployment. One of the most significant areas of concern is the potential for AI systems to exacerbate existing societal inequalities. AI algorithms are trained on data, and if that data reflects existing biases, the resulting AI systems will likely perpetuate and even amplify those biases. For instance, facial recognition systems have been shown to exhibit higher error rates for individuals with darker skin tones, potentially leading to misidentification and unjust consequences in law enforcement and security applications. Similarly, algorithms used in loan applications or hiring processes might discriminate against certain demographic groups if the training data reflects historical biases in lending or hiring practices. Addressing these biases requires careful attention to data collection, preprocessing, and algorithm design, as well as ongoing monitoring and evaluation of AI systems for fairness. Techniques such as fairness-aware machine learning are being developed to mitigate these biases, but the challenge remains significant, demanding continuous research and development.

Beyond bias, AI's impact on employment is a major concern. Automation driven by AI has the potential to displace workers in various industries, from manufacturing and transportation to customer service and data entry. While AI may create new job opportunities in areas like AI development and maintenance, the transition may be challenging for workers whose skills become obsolete. This necessitates proactive measures such as retraining and upskilling programs to equip workers with the skills needed for the jobs of the future. Furthermore, exploring alternative economic models, such as universal basic income, is crucial to mitigate the potential negative consequences of widespread job displacement caused by AI-driven automation.

The ethical considerations surrounding AI in healthcare are also profound. AI systems are increasingly being used for diagnosis, treatment planning, and drug discovery. While these applications hold immense potential for improving healthcare outcomes, they also raise concerns about patient privacy, data security, and algorithmic accountability. Ensuring the confidentiality and security of patient data is paramount, requiring robust security measures and adherence to strict data privacy regulations. Moreover, the potential for errors in AI-driven diagnoses or treatment plans necessitates mechanisms for human oversight and accountability. It is crucial to strike a balance between leveraging the potential of AI to enhance healthcare and mitigating the risks associated with its deployment. Transparency in the decision-making processes of AI systems used in healthcare is also essential to build trust and enable informed consent.

The use of AI in the criminal justice system presents another complex ethical challenge. AI-powered tools are being employed for predictive policing, risk assessment, and sentencing recommendations. However, the use of such tools raises concerns about bias, fairness, and due process. If AI systems are trained on data that reflects historical biases in policing or sentencing, they may perpetuate and amplify those biases, leading to unfair and discriminatory outcomes. The lack of transparency in the algorithms used in these systems further complicates matters, making it difficult to understand how decisions are made and to challenge them.

Ensuring fairness and accountability in the use of AI in the criminal justice system requires rigorous evaluation of these systems for bias, transparency in their operation, and mechanisms for human oversight. Establishing clear ethical guidelines and legal frameworks is crucial to prevent the misuse of AI in this sensitive context.

The spread of misinformation and disinformation facilitated by AI-powered technologies is another significant societal concern. AI can be used to generate realistic-looking fake videos and audio recordings (deepfakes), potentially manipulating public opinion and undermining trust in legitimate sources of information. This raises concerns about the integrity of information and the potential for social unrest. Combating this challenge requires a multifaceted approach involving media literacy education, development of technologies to detect deepfakes, and policies to address the malicious use of AI for creating and disseminating misinformation. Collaboration between researchers, policymakers, and social media platforms is crucial to address this evolving threat.

Autonomous weapons systems (AWS), also known as lethal autonomous weapons, pose perhaps the most significant ethical dilemma. These systems have the potential to make life-or-death decisions without human intervention, raising fundamental questions about accountability, human control, and the potential for unintended consequences. The possibility of malfunction, hacking, or misinterpretation of commands by an AWS raises serious concerns about the safety and security of both combatants and civilians. The absence of human oversight in such systems fundamentally alters the nature of warfare, raising concerns about potential escalation, loss of control, and violation of international humanitarian law. The development and deployment of AWS demand careful consideration of these ethical implications, necessitating international cooperation and the establishment of robust regulatory frameworks to prevent their misuse. A global moratorium on the development and deployment of fully autonomous weapons systems is a crucial step towards preventing a catastrophic arms race and protecting human lives.

The impact of AI on privacy is multifaceted and far-reaching. AI systems often rely on vast amounts of personal data to function effectively. This raises concerns about the collection, storage, and use of sensitive personal information. Ensuring the privacy of individuals in the age of AI requires robust data protection regulations, transparent data handling practices, and mechanisms for individuals to control their data. The development of privacy-preserving AI techniques, such as federated learning and differential privacy, is crucial to mitigate the risks to individual privacy posed by AI systems. It's important to note that the very design of AI systems needs to prioritize privacy from the outset, instead of being an afterthought. This necessitates integrating privacy considerations into the development lifecycle of AI, ensuring that privacy is not just an add-on but a fundamental design principle.

The societal impact of AI is a dynamic and evolving field, requiring continuous research, dialogue, and collaboration. Addressing these challenges requires a multi-stakeholder approach involving researchers, policymakers, industry leaders, and civil society organizations. The development and implementation of ethical guidelines and regulations are crucial for ensuring that AI technologies are developed and used responsibly, benefiting society as a whole while mitigating potential risks. Promoting public understanding of AI and fostering responsible innovation are essential for navigating this complex landscape and ensuring that AI serves humanity's best interests. The future of AI hinges on our ability to proactively address its societal implications, making informed decisions based on ethical principles and a commitment to social good. Continuous learning, adaptation, and a commitment to ethical reflection are crucial for ensuring that this transformative technology benefits society as a whole. Failure to prioritize ethics and responsibility risks undermining trust in AI and creating a world where technology exacerbates existing inequalities and injustices. The ongoing dialogue and collaboration between researchers, developers, policymakers, and the public are essential to navigate this complex landscape effectively. Only through this concerted effort can we harness the potential of AI while mitigating its risks and ensuring a future where this powerful technology serves the common good.

Future Directions and Resources for Continued Learning

The journey into the world of artificial intelligence is a continuous learning process. This book has provided a foundational understanding of AI principles, techniques, and practical applications. However, the field is rapidly evolving, constantly expanding its capabilities and raising new challenges. Therefore, to stay abreast of the latest advancements and deepen your understanding, continued learning is paramount. This section outlines pathways for such continued learning, highlighting key resources and strategies that will empower you to navigate the complexities of AI's future.

One of the most effective methods for continued learning is engaging with the vibrant AI research community. This involves actively participating in online forums, attending conferences and workshops, and subscribing to relevant newsletters and publications. Platforms like arXiv, a repository for pre-print articles, offer immediate access to cutting-edge research across diverse AI subfields. Conferences such as NeurIPS, ICML, and AAAI represent crucial opportunities to learn about the latest breakthroughs directly from leading researchers and engage with peers. These events often feature tutorials and workshops tailored to different experience levels, providing opportunities to delve deeper into specific topics. Many leading research institutions and universities also host public lectures and seminars, offering valuable insights into current research trends and future directions.

Beyond formal academic settings, online learning platforms provide unparalleled accessibility to AI education. Platforms like Coursera, edX, Udacity, and fast.ai offer a wide range of courses on various aspects of AI, from introductory programming to advanced deep learning techniques. These courses often feature interactive exercises, hands-on projects, and assignments, providing opportunities to apply theoretical knowledge to practical scenarios. Many courses are taught by renowned experts in the field, providing invaluable guidance and insights. The flexibility of these online platforms allows for self-paced learning, enabling learners to adjust their pace based on their understanding and availability. This asynchronous learning format is particularly beneficial for those juggling multiple commitments, making it easier to integrate AI education into a busy schedule.

Specific areas to focus your continued learning on include the constantly evolving landscape of deep learning architectures. While this book covered fundamental architectures like CNNs, RNNs, and Transformers, research is constantly pushing the boundaries, leading to the development of new and improved architectures tailored to specific tasks and data types. Keeping up with these advancements requires diligent monitoring of research publications and participation in online discussions within the AI community. Explore papers related to newer architectures like graph neural networks (GNNs) for relational data, capsule networks for better handling of spatial hierarchies, and attention mechanisms beyond Transformers. These developments are constantly impacting various AI applications, particularly in areas like natural language processing, computer vision, and robotics.

Another crucial aspect of continued learning is the practical application of AI techniques. The best way to solidify your understanding is through hands-on projects and real-world applications. Start by working on personal projects that interest you. This could involve building an image classifier for your own collection of photos, developing a chatbot using a large language model, or even building a simple game-playing AI using reinforcement learning techniques. Contributing to open-source projects is another excellent way to gain practical experience and learn from experienced developers. Platforms like GitHub host a plethora of open-source AI projects, offering opportunities to contribute code, fix bugs, and learn from the collaborative efforts of the broader AI community. Participating in Kaggle competitions is also a fantastic way to enhance your skills and test your abilities against a global community of AI enthusiasts.

Understanding and addressing the ethical implications of AI is a critical component of responsible AI development. This book touched on this crucial topic, but dedicated study and ongoing dialogue are essential. Explore resources focused on AI ethics, including academic papers, industry reports, and policy documents. Familiarize yourself with ethical frameworks and guidelines developed by organizations like the IEEE, ACM, and the Partnership on AI. Critically evaluate the societal impact of AI technologies and actively participate in discussions regarding responsible AI practices. This involves staying informed about relevant legislation and regulations and contributing to the development of ethical guidelines and best practices within your own work and community. Participating in workshops and conferences dedicated to AI ethics and responsible innovation is highly beneficial.

Finally, mastering the art of lifelong learning is essential in the rapidly evolving field of AI. The skills and knowledge you acquire today may become outdated relatively quickly, necessitating a commitment to continuous learning and adaptation. Develop strategies for staying current with new developments. This might involve setting aside dedicated time each week to read research papers, attend webinars, or take online courses. Cultivate a habit of continuous learning by integrating it into your daily routine, even in small increments. Embrace the challenge of learning new technologies and adapting to evolving methodologies. The field of AI is dynamic, and a commitment to lifelong learning is the only way to truly master its complexities and contribute effectively to its progress.

To further aid your journey, here are some specific resources categorized for easier navigation:

Online Courses:

Coursera:
Offers courses on various aspects of AI, from introductory levels to advanced specializations. Look for courses from top universities like Stanford, MIT, and deeplearning.ai.
edX:
Similar to Coursera, edX provides high-quality courses taught by renowned academics and industry experts.
Udacity:
Specializes in more practical and project-based learning, often with nanodegree programs for focused skill development.
fast.ai:
Offers practical and approachable courses on deep learning, targeting both beginners and experienced practitioners.

Research Repositories & Publications:

arXiv:
A pre-print server hosting a vast collection of research papers in AI and related fields.
ACM Digital Library:
A comprehensive archive of
academic publications in computer science, including many important AI papers.

IEEE Xplore:
Another extensive digital library covering a broad range of engineering disciplines, with a significant

section on AI.

Nature Machine Intelligence:
A leading journal publishing cutting-edge research in AI and its applications.

Science Robotics:
Focuses on robotics-related AI research.

Conferences & Workshops:

NeurIPS (Neural Information Processing Systems):
One of the most prestigious AI conferences, attracting leading researchers worldwide.

ICML (International Conference on Machine Learning):
Another top-tier conference focused on machine learning algorithms and theory.

AAAI (Association for the Advancement of Artificial Intelligence):
A leading organization for AI research, hosting conferences and workshops on various topics.

Open-Source Projects & Communities:

GitHub:
Host to a vast number of open-source AI projects. Search for projects relevant to your interests and contribute to their development.

Kaggle:
A platform for data science competitions, providing opportunities to test your skills and collaborate with other AI enthusiasts.

By actively engaging with these resources and fostering a culture of continuous learning, you will be well-equipped to navigate the exciting and ever-evolving landscape of artificial intelligence. Remember, the journey is ongoing; the more you learn, the more you will discover, and the more you will contribute to shaping the future of this transformative technology. Embrace the challenge, stay curious, and never stop learning. The future of AI is being built today, and your contributions are invaluable.

Acknowledgments

First and foremost, I would like to express my sincere gratitude to my family for their unwavering support and patience throughout the long process of writing this book. Their encouragement and understanding were instrumental in bringing this project to fruition.
I would also want to thank the countless individuals who have contributed to the field of artificial intelligence, whose work and insights form the foundation of this book. Their research, innovation, and dedication have made it possible to create this comprehensive guide.

Appendix

This appendix provides supplementary materials to enhance your understanding of the concepts covered in the book. It includes:

A1: Detailed Installation Instructions for Different Operating Systems:
This section offers step-by-step instructions for setting up your AI development environment on Windows, macOS, and Linux systems, addressing potential installation issues specific to each platform.

A2: Solutions to Selected Exercises:
This section provides solutions to a selection of exercises presented throughout the book to help you check your understanding and identify areas for improvement.

A3: Advanced Topics in Neural Networks:
This section briefly explores more advanced neural network architectures and techniques, including Generative Adversarial Networks (GANs) and Autoencoders, providing further avenues for exploration.

A4: Python Cheat Sheet:
A quick reference guide summarizing essential Python syntax and functions used throughout the book.

A5: Datasets Used in the Book:
Links to download all the datasets used for practical projects and examples throughout the book.

Glossary

This glossary provides definitions for key terms used throughout "AI from Scratch."

Activation Function:
A function applied to the output of a neuron to introduce non-linearity into the network. Examples include sigmoid, ReLU, and tanh.

Backpropagation:
An algorithm used to train neural networks by calculating the gradient of the loss function with respect to the network's weights.

Bias-Variance Tradeoff:
The balance between a model's ability to fit the training data (bias) and its ability to generalize to unseen data (variance).

Convolutional Neural Network (CNN):
A type of neural network designed for processing grid-like data, particularly images.

Deep Learning:
A subfield of machine learning that uses artificial neural networks with multiple layers to learn complex patterns from data.

Gradient Descent:
An iterative optimization algorithm used to find the minimum of a function by following the direction of the negative gradient.

Hyperparameters:
Parameters that control the learning process of a machine learning model, such as learning rate and number of epochs.

Machine Learning:
A field of study that gives computers the ability to learn without being explicitly programmed.

Recurrent Neural Network (RNN):
A type of neural
network designed for processing sequential data, such as text and time series.

Reinforcement Learning:
A type of machine learning where an agent learns to interact with an environment by receiving rewards and penalties.

References

Author Biography

Scott Johnsey has always been interested in Artificial Intelligence. From the early beginning of movies and TV show, to the theories of how to make it happen, and now the infant level of AI that it has grown into, he has kept a curious mind and sharp eye on all of the advancements. With hopes of smart design and careful planning, Scott welcomes the future of AI into normal everyday life.

www.ingramcontent.com/pod-product-compliance
Lightning Source LLC
Chambersburg PA
CBHW052142220526
45471CB00004B/1480